10 TREASURE LEGENDS!

ARIZONA

Lost Gold, Hidden Hoards and Fantastic Fortunes

10 LOST TREASURES: *Arizona*

Commander - J. Hutton Pulitzer, CC, CSA, CSI, ACE

Cover Design and Book Layout by Christopher Cline

Table of Contents

CHAPTER ONE

HISTORY HUNTERS OR HISTORY LOOTERS?

Artifact Rescuers or Archaeological Racists?

CHAPTER 1 HISTORY HUNTERS OR HISTORY LOOTERS?

"Could imagine nothing pleasanter than to spend all of our lives digging for relics of the past"
-Heinrich Schliemann

Controversy is boiling around the term "Treasure Hunter" or "Treasure Hunting". Regularly I get into online group debates over the use of the term "Treasure Hunter". It actually sickens me to see people arbitrarily classify the two words "treasure hunter" as a "grave robber" and as something illegal. Personally, I liken the term "looter" to the term "racist" and here is what I mean by that.

In the Archaeological community people have been trained to scream "looter" at anyone who is treasure hunting, history hunting, metal detecting or artifact collecting. The reason they scream "looter" is because it tends to put people immediately on the defensive and it gives the one screaming "looter" the upper hand because they then control the conversation, debate and/or discussion (although there is very little discussion and mostly screaming and drowning out by those yelling "looter"). The exact thing happens when someone calls another person "racist". They immediately put the other party on the defensive and in most cases all one can do is start to back off from their position and immediately start apologizing. In other words, calling someone a "looter" or a "racist" is a word used to shut people up immediately or force an apology or backing off from their position, with no regard if the actual position has merit to begin with.

As for me, when that word is "screamed at me online" (I say that because it is usually a single post of that word is in **ALL CAPS**, which is the online equivalent of yelling at someone), very often, but in my usual style I do not back off and always answer every accusation with compelling facts supporting my stance. Invariably more often than not, the group admin – who is most likely an academic involved in the Archaeological community clicks that virtual button to shut me up. What is that virtual shut-someone-up button? The "Ban from Group" button. By banning one and shutting down debate or discussion, they feel doing such gives them the last word. They almost always continue on in the group among themselves bashing me and all treasure hunters and there is not a thing we can do to rebut the accusations. Thus the cycle of misinformation continues to dig deeper into the overall consciousness.

Sometimes, and not the norm at all and not more of an actual end result of more than 1% of all these online debates (or debates against the counter opinion of the group), the group will actually find a mutual ground with me – a horrible Treasure Hunter or History Hunter – and they agree to disagree but let the participation in the group continue. That is the way it should be, since freedom of speech is something to be cherished, supported and honored; if not for it being the right thing to do but the honorable thing to do in honoring the millions in history who have fought wars and died for this basic right. Freedom of Speech.

Here is how I usually fight this fight head on and at least stimulate a helpful and healthy debate of the issue of whether one is a "History Hunter" or "History Looter" an "Artifact Rescuer" or an "Archaeological Racist".

What has happened is the archaeological community has forgotten and shunned its roots (something I deal with as a Jew and the Jewish people shunning their roots and hating everything Jewish, but that is another topic all together). The system has turned on itself and started to devour itself, but has not come out the other end and totally reinvented itself yet. The inevitable "Phoenix rising from the ashes". There is a "reinvented solution" (I will share it a few chapters forward) that already exists today for this problem; but here in the United States this "reinvention" has not occurred yet and unfortunately the result is both hard to interpret laws and laws with unintended consequences (or intended consequences depending which side of the debate you come down on).

This cycle has a symbol and the symbol is called the "Ouroboros".

The Ouroboros or Uroboros (/jʊərəˈbɒrəs/; /ɔːˈrɒbərəs/, from the Greek οὐροβόρος ὄφις tail-devouring snake) is an ancient symbol depicting a serpent or dragon eating its own tail.

Often symbolizes self-reflexivity or cyclicality, especially in the sense of something constantly re-creating itself, the eternal return, and other things such as the phoenix which operate in cycles that begin anew as soon as they end. It can also represent the idea of primordial unity related to something existing in or persisting from the beginning with such force or qualities it cannot be extinguished. While first emerging in Ancient Egypt, it has been important in religious and mythological symbolism, but has also been frequently used in alchemical illustrations, where it symbolizes the circular nature of the alchemist's opus. It is also often associated with Gnosticism, and Hermeticism.

So to understand both the problem and the "solution to and of" the "History Hunter" versus "History Looter" or "Artifact Rescuer" versus "Archaeological Racists" we have to go back in time and understand the beginnings of an industry first.

CHAPTER TWO

"FROM THE MOUTHS OF BABES".

An industry built from the imagination and determination of an 8 year old who loved books!

"My sole and only aim is to be able to establish a historical fact, on which I disagree with some eminent historians and geographers"

-Heinrich Schliemann

What a lot of hobbyist do not know and most academic professionals choose to ignore, is that the profession and educational institution of Archaeology all began with (insert dramatic drum roll here) a "History Hunter" who was ultimately called a "History Looter", who was really an "Artifact Rescuer" but the industry he birthed all became "Archaeological Racist" and now they either ignore or demonize their founding father! Chances are you have never come across the photograph below.

This man's name is Heinrich Schliemann. You, Me, Archaeologists, Historians, Anthropologist, Cultural Geography, Cultural Studies, Antiquities, Historiography, Comparative Literature, Etymologists and almost 50 other educational and scientific fields of study, owe this man – A GERMAN GROCER - a thank you and a place of honor in history (but that would take supporting facts and truth and not academic oriented half-truths. Again, another whole different story).

Unfortunately the ones (Archaeologists) who should really honor Heinrich Schliemann, those who have their many accredited degrees to thank him for, actually detest and debase the man. A great man, who did great things and did mankind, academics, history and education a great favor. What was that favor he did?

Heinrich Schliemann believed that history as we knew it and were told was WRONG and he used his own funds to go out to find and prove TRUE HISTORY and the actual ARTIFACTS TO PROVE IT.

Is that a "History Hunter" OR "History Looter" or "Artifact Rescuer" REVILED BY "Archaeological Racists"? You decide. To me the answer is obvious, but here is the shortened version for you to file away in your brain and use when you come up against the very same critics and criticism.

Heinrich's Wiki Background: Schliemann was born in Neubukow, Mecklenburg-Schwerin in 1822. His father, Ernst Schliemann, was a Protestant minister. The family moved to Ankershagen in 1823 (today in their house is the museum of Heinrich Schliemann). Heinrich's mother, Luise Therese Sophie, died in 1831, when Heinrich was nine years old.

10

After his mother's death his father sent Heinrich to live with his uncle. When he was eleven years old his father paid for him to enroll in the Gymnasium (grammar school) at Neustrelitz. Heinrich's later interest in history was initially encouraged by his father who had schooled him in the tales of the Iliad and the Odyssey and had given him a copy of Ludwig Jerrer's Illustrated History of the World for Christmas in 1829. Thus, his passion for Homer was born.

Schliemann at the age of 8, declared he would one day find and prove the city of Troy really existed!

However, Heinrich had to transfer to the Realschule (vocational school), since his family could not afford private schooling. His family's poverty made a university education impossible, so it was Schliemann's early academic experiences that influenced the course of his education as an adult. In later years, the industry he spawned and the actual academic degrees which were created as a direct result of his work and techniques

(Archaeologist); would shun his historic legacy as the industry's creator because he himself did not have a University degree.

At age 14, after leaving Realschule, Heinrich became an apprentice at Herr Holtz's grocery in Fürstenberg. He labored for five years until he was forced to leave because he burst a blood vessel lifting a heavy barrel. In 1841, Schliemann moved to Hamburg and became a cabin boy on the Dorothea, a steamer bound for Venezuela. After twelve days at sea, the ship foundered in a gale. The survivors washed up on the shores of the Netherlands. Schliemann became a messenger, office attendant, and later, a bookkeeper in Amsterdam.

On March 1, 1844, 22-year old Schliemann took a position with B. H. Schröder & Co., an import/export firm. In 1846 the firm sent him as a General Agent to St. Petersburg. In time, Schliemann represented a number of companies. He learned Russian and Greek, employing a system that he used his entire life to learn languages—Schliemann's skills allowed him to learn a new language within six weeks and wrote his diary in the language of whatever country he happened to be in.

By the end of his life, Schliemann could converse in English, French, Dutch, Spanish, Portuguese, Swedish, Polish, Italian, Greek, Latin, Russian, Arabic, and Turkish as well as German, unlike most academics at the time who only spoke Queen's English and shunned other languages. Schliemann's ability with languages was an important part of his career as a businessman in the importing trade.

In 1850, Heinrich learned of the death of his brother, Ludwig, who had become wealthy as a speculator in the California gold fields. Schliemann went to California in early 1851 and started a bank in Sacramento buying and reselling over a million dollars of gold dust in just six months. While he was there, California became the 31st state in September 1850 and Schliemann acquired United States citizenship. On April 7, 1852, he sold his business and returned to Russia. There he lived the life of a gentleman and met Ekaterina Lyschin, the niece of one of his wealthy friends.

Heinrich and Ekaterina married on October 12, 1852. Schliemann then cornered the market in indigo dye and went into the indigo business itself, turning a good profit. Ekaterina and Heinrich had a son, Sergey, and two daughters, Natalya and Nadezhda, born in 1855, 1858 and 1861 respectively. Schliemann, an entrepreneur at heart, made yet another fortune as a military contractor in the Crimean War, 1854-1856. He cornered the market in saltpeter, sulfur, and lead, constituents of ammunition, which he resold to the Russian government.

By 1858, Schliemann was wealthy enough to retire and decided to dedicate himself to the pursuit of Troy.

CHAPTER THREE

THE PRIVATELY FUNDED TREASURE HUNT THAT STARTED IT ALL!

The photo above is called the "Mask of Agamemnon" and it is one of the most well-known and recognized photos of treasure ever published. Look at that amazing artifact that was RESCUED from obscurity by someone who had the passion, funds and took the time to research and find it! A person not classically trained who wanted to prove up history, correct historical wrongs and bring precious artifacts to LIFE which were potentially buried in the earth for millennia! Sounds a lot like you and the people you metal detect, treasure hunt and ghost town explore with, doesn't it? Real people with real passions going the extra mile.

Back to Schliemann's story as recorded by Wiki:

Schliemann's first interest of a classical nature seems to have been the location of Troy.

At the time Schliemann began excavating in Turkey, the site commonly believed to be Troy was at Pınarbaşı, a hilltop at the south end of the Trojan Plain. In 1868, Schliemann visited sites in the Greek world, published Ithaka, der Peloponnesus und Troja in which he asserted that Hissarlik was the site of Troy, and submitted a dissertation in Ancient Greek proposing the same thesis to the University of Rostock. In 1869, he was awarded a PhD from the University of Rostock for that submission.

The 'Mask of Agamemnon', discovered by Heinrich Schliemann in 1876 at Mycenae now exhibited at the National Archaeological Museum of Athens.

By this time divorced from his wife and working exclusively abroad, Schliemann needed an assistant who was knowledgeable in matters pertaining to Greek culture. A friend, the Archbishop of Athens, suggested a relative of his, Sophia Engastromenos (1852–1932). They married in October 1869. They later had two children, Andromache and Agamemnon Schliemann

Schliemann began work on Troy in 1871. His excavations began before archaeology was even called archaeology and could even be considered something valuable enough for academic accreditation and study. As a direct result of Schliemann's work and success, archaeology developed into a professional field.

A cache of gold and other objects appeared in May 1873; Schliemann named it "Priam's Treasure". He later wrote that he had seen the gold glinting in the dirt and dismissed the workmen so that he and Sophia could excavate it themselves, removing it in her shawl. Sophia later wore "the Jewels of Helen" for the public. Those jewels, taken from the Pergamon Museum in Berlin by the Soviet Army (Red Army) in 1945, are now in the Pushkin Museum in Moscow.

Schliemann published his findings in 1874, in Trojanische Altertümer ("Trojan Antiquities").

This publicity backfired when the Turkish government revoked Schliemann's permission to dig and sued him for a share of the gold. Schliemann smuggled the treasure out of Turkey. He defended his "moving of the artifacts out of Turkey" as an attempt to protect the items from corrupt local officials.

Schliemann published Troja und seine Ruinen (Troy and Its Ruins) in 1875 and excavated the Treasury of Minyas at Orchomenus. In 1876, he began digging at Mycenae. Upon discovering the Shaft Graves, with their skeletons and more regal gold (including the Mask of Agamemnon), Schliemann cabled the king of Greece. The results were published in Mykenai in 1878.

Although he had received permission in 1876 to continue excavation, Schliemann did not reopen the dig site at Troy until 1878–1879, after another excavation in Ithaca designed to locate an actual site mentioned in the Odyssey. On August 1, 1890, Schliemann returned reluctantly to Athens, and in November travelled to Halle, where a long persistent chronic ear infection was operated upon. On November 13, the doctors deemed the operation a success, but his inner ear became painfully inflamed. Ignoring his doctors' advice, he left the hospital and travelled to Leipzig, Berlin, and Paris. From the latter, he planned to return to Athens in time for Christmas, but his ear condition became even worse. Too sick to make the boat ride from Naples to Greece, Schliemann remained in Naples, but managed to make a journey to the ruins of Pompeii. On Christmas Day he collapsed into a coma and died in a Naples hotel room on December 26, 1890.

The cause of death was cholesteatoma. His corpse was then transported by friends to the First Cemetery in Athens. It was interred in a mausoleum shaped like a temple erected in ancient Greek style designed by Ernst Ziller in the form of a pedimental sculpture. The frieze circling the outside of the mausoleum shows Schliemann conducting the excavations at Mycenae and other sites. His magnificent residence in the city center of Athens, houses today the Numismatic Museum of AthensNow that you have the background story of the man who actually discovered the discipline of Archaeology, here is what the Archaeological industry now projects to the world about their founding father- Heinrich Schliemann:

(1) In 1972, Professor William Calder of the University of Colorado, speaking at a commemoration of Schliemann's birthday, claimed that he had *uncovered several possible problems in Schliemann's work*. Other investigators followed, such as Professor David Traill of the University of California.

(2) An article published by the National Geographic Society called into question Schliemann's qualifications, his motives, and his methods.

(3) *"In northwestern Turkey, Heinrich Schliemann excavated the site believed to be Troy in 1870. Schliemann was a German adventurer and con man who took sole credit for the discovery, even though he was digging at the site, called Hisarlik, at the behest of British archaeologist Frank Calvert. ... Eager to find the legendary treasures of Troy, Schliemann blasted his way down to the second city, where he found what he believed were the jewels that once belonged to Helen. As it turns out, the jewels were a thousand years older than the time described in Homer's epic".*

(NOTE: There was NO SUCH accreditation as Archaeologist, yet the above calls Frank Calvert -who was doing the same as Schliemann, but was not successful- an Archaeologist. Why? Calvert was English and considered a Gentlemen – and he did not have a degree either, yet he is called an Archaeologist and Schliemann is called an "uneducated con-man". This type of attempt at discrediting is still deployed today against anyone not an Archaeologist and considered a "Treasure Hunter" - Welcome to the world of Archeological and Academic Racism! Another article presented similar criticisms when reporting on a speech by University of Pennsylvania scholar C. Brian Rose:

(4) *"German archaeologist Heinrich Schliemann was the first to explore the Mound of Troy in the 1870s. Unfortunately, he had had no formal education in archaeology, and dug an enormous trench "which we still call the Schliemann Trench," according to Rose, because in the process Schliemann "destroyed a phenomenal amount of material." "Only much later in his career would he accept the fact that the treasure had been found at a layer one thousand years removed from the battle between the Greeks and Trojans, and thus that it could not have been the treasure of King Priam. Schliemann may not have discovered the truth, but the publicity stunt worked, making Schliemann and the site famous and igniting the field of Homeric studies in the late 19th century".*

Talk about spitting in the face and on the history of the individual who personally, with his own funds, developed and launched the industry of Archaeology. No matter how it is put, to undertake searching and digging – private or professional – they require funding. In Schliemann's day the adventure was a sport of wealthy individuals looking for history, fame and fortune.

Here is an interesting fact: You've heard of King Tut right? It's founder, Howard Carter? Here is what Wiki and many sites say about Carter- *"Howard Carter (9 May 1874 – 2 March 1939) was an English archaeologist and Egyptologist who became world famous after discovering the intact tomb of 14th-century BC pharaoh Tutankhamun (colloquially known as "King Tut" and "the boy king")"*

Interesting fact: Carter went to Egypt at the age of 17, had no University education, but was able to go to Egypt because of family ties and being English and what do we "see" in the academic record? Carter is called both an Archaeologist and Egyptologist. See the trend? If you are "in" the right circles and from the right breeding, history will apply an advanced degree upon you and refer to you as "the degreed"; but be from nothing- an entrepreneur and out to prove history and academics wrong – you are branded a con-man, scammer or scoundrel. These are the facts, when presented to the archaeological community which enrage modern day archaeologists when used to defend treasure hunting and history hunting.

However, in an ironic turn of events, the British finally came full circle and were reborn better (remember the Ouroboros?). The Ouroboros I shared with you earlier - means to be reborn and what has happened is the country that held itself above all other people and races – especially in education and academic circles; has now become enlightened and figured out a system where both the private hunters and the archaeological accredited can co-exist and work well together.

Here is how it works in the United Kingdom (it is a great blue print):

1. All citizens can metal detect and treasure hunt and it is encouraged!

2. Why is it encouraged? There are more citizens than academics. Simple math.

3. Citizen makes a find

4. Citizen reports the find to the local Coroner (yes like the crime scene guys that pronounce the dead and cart away the dead bodies)

5. Coroner notifies the Crown

6. Crown funds the dig and restoration and AS SUCH they employ Archaeologist, Historians, Anthropologists and all kinds of academics.

7. Crown cleans up and restores the finds

8. Crown get three professional appraisals of the value of the find

9. Crown takes the appraisals average and determines value – let's say $2,000,000.

10. Crown pays the $2,000,000 to the finder and /or landowner (they split the funds)

11. Crowns thanks the finder profusely and even writes stories about them an makes them mini-celebrities

12. Crown keeps the find and puts them on public display in Museum

Did you catch that? Everyone one wins! This is the perfect win/win.

But what do American academics do? The SAME that third world countries do! Make it a crime and put people in prison – if they can. Now it is understandable why third world countries and dictators do this. They are greedy, want to sell off the treasure and pocket the funds and continue to steal from the people. But why does the United States of America do this?

The simple fact is because two issues collide.

One: Academics gets tenure and bigger University paychecks **IF** they get published and make great finds! But there is a problem.

Two: Universities no longer pay for exploration. Seems to of died in the fictional character "Indiana Jones" time period (how ironic).

Here is the conundrum: How can an Academic Archaeologist get raises, professional praise and accolades IF they institution they work for does not even pay for exploration?

It's simple, they help write laws that keep regular Joe's and Joann's from metal detecting and treasure hunting. Why? They cannot let the individual make finds because it does not benefit "me-the academic" and thus "I don't get tenure or accolades". So here is what they want.

One: You find it (although you are not supposed to)

Two: You tell them exactly where it is and give them proof of it

Three: Then "they" get you banned from the site and threaten to get you imprisoned

Four: If you have not told them the location, they try to coerce you into it so you want to save your "ass" from legal troubles

Five: They (the archaeologists and academics) then go to the site and IF something is really there, they get state and academic funds (why now? Because YOU proved it was there) and they start digging

Six: They don't get the "money from the find" so what they do (under the guise it take a lot of time) they extract fees, salaries and cost dragging out the excavation out for years and or decades (job security)

Seven: Once finished they write a book, get huge press, awards and accolades and THEY are "the discoverer" of the "find". Your name is never mentioned. I know, and they call YOU the one STEALING AND LOOTING. It's not the Seven Deadly Sins – it's the Seven Ways One Can Steal Finds Legally!

Yep, our U.S. system is messed up, but one day the system might become enlightened and embracing and learn that there are millions of people who will scour every inch of land in the US, if the system who not threaten them, would give them credit and incentive and then the **TWO DIFFERENT SYSTEMS** become partners. Now that works and the British proved it.

Happy Hunting and as always know the laws and rules and have a grand adventure!

BUT, before we get to the 10 Treasure Legends, I am going to do a little bit of a refresher from some of my earlier writings so you can understand both the nature of Treasure Legends and the facts and fictions that always surround them.

So, just a little refresher course, because with at least a little bit of understanding of how to find treasure, then maybe the reading experience will be that much better for you.

CHAPTER FOUR

MILLIONS, BILLIONS, OR TRILLIONS?

Billions of dollars in lost treasure waiting to be found? That figure must seem outrageous, or at the very least incorrect? If you wondered this to yourself, then you are actually right. There are not billions of dollars out there in lost treasures waiting to be reclaimed. There are trillions of dollars of treasure waiting to be reclaimed. But, I was faced with making a choice when it came to publishing this book. Would I be able to convince the public at large there were millions or even billions to recover, much less trillions? I chose the middle road, a number far more conservative than any realistic assessment. Why?

Most people, right off the top of their heads, could **NOT** tell you how many zeros are in one trillion.

Well, one trillion is 1,000,000,000,000. **1 2 3 4 5 6 7 8 9 10 11 12** - that's **twelve** zeroes.

In fact, to give you a better perspective, in the state of Texas alone, where I am sitting as I write this, there is an estimated $99,581,605,263 (ninety-nine billion) in documented unrecovered lost treasures. Compare that to Florida at $201,608,423,684 (two hundred and one billion) or New Mexico at $365,684,242,105 (three hundred and sixty-five billion) and you can easily see how the numbers rack up. But this is still not quite correct.

The numbers for this book were figured using the daily average price of gold on a day over four months ago. Now, as of this writing, gold is up an additional 32%; this means that Texas treasure is worth $31,866,113,684.16 (thirty-one billion) more, while Florida's treasure is worth an extra $64,514,695,578.88 (sixty-four billion) and New Mexico's an extra $117,018,957,473.60 (one hundred seventeen billion).

Absolutely boggles the mind, does it not? You will learn more about these numbers and where they come from in this book. But first and foremost, this book is not about the values of lost treasures now or in the past, but rather the passion and lore that goes into treasure hunting. If you understand history and treasure and the nature of both, you are moving along the road toward becoming a real treasure hunter. Men have sought out the lost, hidden, stored, and cached treasures of others from the beginning of time. Treasure hunting is thousands of years older than the profession of archaeology, and in fact it is the pursuit of treasure that birthed the profession of archaeology.

There are many forms of treasure seekers, from those who seek documents to those who seek artifacts and mineral sources, since treasure itself comes in many forms. In fact, there are papers and books that have been lost to time which are now as valuable as a ton of gold!

30

There are many different levels of seekers as well. There are the treasure seekers who do it for recreation, those who do it for adventure, and those who do it to shore up historical research. The rarest of the treasure seekers are those who make up the professional class of treasure hunters: those who shun the name treasure hunter, due to the modern implications of that label, and who have gone to the trouble of both the education and certification to become what is professionally called **Cacheologists**.

Cacheology:

The profession whereby highly trained and certified individuals, using archaeological methods combined with forensic historical research and modern technology, set out to prove or disprove, dispel or recover, set the historical record straight or professionally document, the various types of caches, common treasures or otherwise, that have been lost to history and mankind. The mission of the Cacheologists is to use profit-driven methods to recover lost caches for the expansion of mankind's study, education, instruction, collection, showcasing, and preservation. Cacheology is the professional rescue and preservation of caches that time and the environment would otherwise rapidly and thoroughly destroy, erasing historical records and artifacts vital and irreplaceable for the entire world.

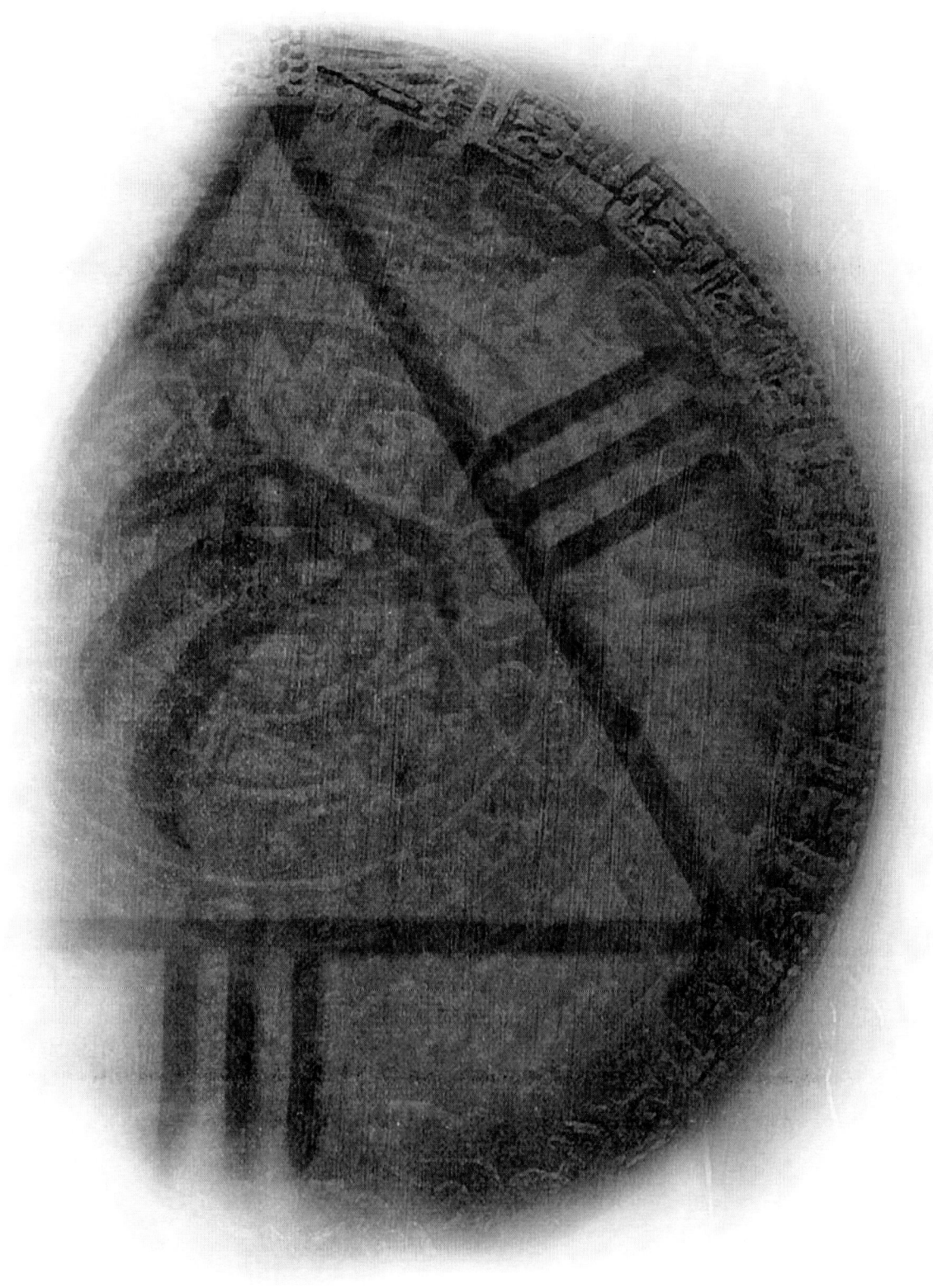

CHAPTER FIVE

CACHEOLOGY

Any Treasure is in fact a cache. A cache is some form of valuables that has been stored, either willingly or under duress, but which was never retrieved. There various forms of caches as well. They are as follows:

1. Cache of *Ceremony*
2. Cache of *Convenience*
3. Cache of *Catastrophe*
4. Cache of *Duress*
5. Cache of *Criminal Activity*
6. Cache of *Nature*

If you understand the nature of a cache, or in other words, if you understand how the cache originally became a cache, you then have a better chance of verifying, locating, and recovering the cache. Below I will give you the formal Cacheological definition of each of these different types of caches, but as you read this book, bear in mind that if you can learn to identify the type of a particular cache, you may have what it takes to become a professional treasure hunter.

CACHE OF CEREMONY

A Cache of Ceremony is the style of cache that has been deposited where it was found (or is yet to be found) due to the nature of the culture and ceremonies that generated the cache to begin with. For example, the treasure of King Tut is exactly this type of cache. Ancient Egyptians buried their dead kings with all of their treasures. Their culture, ceremonies, and religious protocols demanded such; thus, the treasure of King Tut is a Cache of Ceremony. So the rule of thumb for a cache identified as a Cache of Ceremony is: If it was the cultural norm for priests, rulers, and/or notables to be buried in a specific religious or ceremonial style and location, then when you find those you will find the cache. Understand and re-create the ceremony and you can locate the cache.

CACHE OF CONVENIENCE

Convenience is exactly that, where it was convenient to store the cache. These caches were not moved from place to place; they were just stored for convenience. It is also the type of cache utilized by workers, common men, and lay people. Why? There are no ceremonies or cultural standards involved in dictating where to stash the cache. For example, it is said there was more money cached away during the Great Depression than there was stored in banks, and billions and billions of that is still cached in the same hiding places. During the Great Depression, people did not trust banks, so they stored their money, valuables and gold in places only known to them, but surely convenient to them. Those places would be in fencepost holes, water wells, fireplaces, floorboards, and such. Another Cache of Convenience, which actually goes hand in hand with a Cache of Catastrophe (defined below), is anywhere a large battle took place. How? Think of the thousands and thousands of soldiers and warriors in time past that would go to war. Along with them they carried their pay (they could not transfer funds to banks back and forth like we did) and their rings, body ornaments, metals, and religious statuaries. Most of these were various forms of precious metals. Before battle, but near the troops actual staging area or camp, each soldier would conveniently (there is that word again) bury his or her personal belongings and fortunes before going into battle. This way they were assured not to lose them and their personal caches would not fall into the hands of the enemy.

Now consider just how many of the warriors would not come back from the battle. Of course, these caches were put there by the attacking army, not any city which was attacked by surprise. So, especially due to invading Roman armies, there are hundreds of thousands, if not millions, of personal soldier or warrior caches in and around camps, staging areas and battlegrounds. 10,000 dead warriors add up to tons of recovered cache troves in each battle area.

CACHE OF CATASTROPHE

Catastrophe is a harsh word. A harsh word for harsh circumstances. Disaster, war, earthquake, shipwreck: chose any word that means that people and their places and/or modes of transport are destroyed, then you understand the concept of Cache of Catastrophe.

Spanish and Chinese treasure ships going down in hurricanes are Caches of Catastrophe. Where the catastrophe happened is where the cache was deposited. An ancient temple or library destroyed by a massive earthquake and dropped off into the sea to never be seen again is a Cache of Catastrophe, and where the catastrophe happened, the cache lays in wait for the Cacheologist.

Understand the nature and scope of the catastrophe and you can locate the cache, but remember, by its very nature a Cache of Catastrophe is either at the bottom of the ocean or buried under tons and tons of ancient debris covered in turn by the debris and buildup of time. These caches may be fairly easy to locate but very hard and expensive to recover.

CACHE OF DURESS

Logically you might question, "What is really the difference between duress and catastrophe?" The simple answer is **SURVIVAL**. Yes, an unexpected attack of an army or Indians is a catastrophe, and those things and people caught up in the catastrophe ultimately lay exactly where the catastrophe happened. But what about the survivors? There are almost always survivors; how else would we know the historical facts, places, people, and issues, except from those that survived. Indian attacks, routed armies, and flight from pursuers are all causes of caches of duress.

Now put yourself in the survivors' situation. All hell is breaking loose. You grab your family and valuables and haul ass. Literally. The survivor is running away from the catastrophe and invariably the transport of their valuables become too much and they hurriedly bury or conceal their cache to be retrieved later. The outlaws with the posse on their tail does not get the gold or bankroll back to their lair or hideout, they have pursuers right behind them, and they hurriedly bury or stash the cache. They don't have the time or luxury to hide the cache very deep or with much sophistication, or to make sure it's not detectable if someone were to come across it.

So, due to the fact that Caches of Duress are survivors or those on the run from imminent danger, the caches they hide are done hurriedly and on the run, and therefore are not deep or very well hidden. These may be the easiest caches to recover, but due to the nature of the situation, they can be spread over a very large area and may in fact be smaller, though not necessarily less valuable. Find the paths taken by those fleeing and along the way you may find many a cache.

CACHE OF CRIMINAL ACTIVITY

Criminals have patterns, partners, and hide outs. Understand those and you understand where to find Caches of Criminal Activity. Yes, in Caches of Duress, I spoke of bandits on the run, so were they not criminals as well, and shouldn't they be listed here? Yes and no. The key is full understanding of the nature of the cache. Yes, the bandit was a criminal, but in that instance, thus the nature of the cache you are seeking, the criminal was on the run being pursued. Therefore they did not reach their hideout, partners in crime, or territory, and they were forced to act under duress.

Remember, understand the nature of the cache and you can find where it is. If you are searching for a trove of gold stolen by Jesse James, and you know that he stole it, fled, and was apprehended (only to escape later), but no gold was found with him, the facts tell you — no, scream to you — that it was stashed on the run. So, do not waste your time looking at his family home or favorite hideout for that particular treasure. But look into the gangsters, bandits, criminals, and drug lords who got away with their ill-gotten goods, and chances are the cache is hidden within their associated network of lairs, hideouts, properties, and partners' properties.

Criminals are notorious for protecting their hidden hoards, and in order to do so the criminal must be within eyeshot, hearing, or quick response distance from the cache. Thus, know the nature of the cache and you can find the cache.

CACHE OF NATURE

Gold, platinum, diamonds, sapphires, and such, do not necessarily have to be mined, minted, and shaped into a royal crown to be considered treasure. Nature is the single largest hider and hoarder of caches. Mother Nature is the single richest individual in the world. Bill Gates and Warren Buffet don't even come a close second to her. Mother Nature is so loaded with treasure she can afford to deposit a trillion dollars in gold or diamonds in a single location and never go back to retrieve them, much less expose them, for millions of years. Most treasure hunters forget this source of wealth, but the professional, the Cacheologist is trained to find these caches as well. In fact, to the Cacheologists, this form of cache is considered low-hanging fruit and ends up being the source of funding for their formal cache expeditions.

Millions upon millions of Caches of Nature exist and someone, somewhere in history has stumbled across them and left us a record and facts to follow. The only thing that happened is the original discoverer of the cache could not remember or relocate the exact location of the cache and therefore could never retrieve it. The easiest example of this is the tons of legends and historical facts surrounding lost gold mines. At some point in time, a prospector came across one of Mother Nature's cache hiding places, but by not paying close attention to their surrounding landmarks or through other circumstances, the prospector went into the nearest town to file their claim, get help, or get supplies and tools and could not find their way back to the natural cache site. There is no way to really put a value on these types of caches because one single cache of nature could be worth a trillion dollars in today's precious metals market, and there are literally thousands upon thousands of these found but lost again Caches of Nature.

But following the clues Mother Nature leaves and stories in the historical record of finds, one could find billions in a single location. If you don't believe me, just ask our Canadian friend and diamond expert, Mr. Fripke. Understand the nature of the cache and you can find the cache.

CHAPTER SIX

FILL IN THE BLANKS AND FIND YOUR FORTUNE!

One of most common questions someone asks when they find out you are a **Professional Treasure Hunter or Cacheologist, is: "What does it take to be able to find lost treasure?"** For me the answer is always the same. Even though we use some sophisticated equipment, venture into dangerous environments and brave terrains and situations most people would never venture into, the **KEY** to successful treasure hunting and recovery is (and in my mind will always be) **GREAT RESEARCH**.

GREAT RESREARCH, that's it. Great research is over 90% of the successful treasure hunting process. No special equipment or special physical prowess will ever replace good old fashioned research. Now, for the first time in the history of humanity, we have more research tools and abilities at our fingertips. Yes, sometimes you do have to travel to an area and go to the local records or tax office to find the information you seek, but now most of what you need to research is only as far as your computer.

Think of a computer or your home computer as the most valuable treasure hunting tool you have. My Grandmother died at the age of 103. I would have many conversations with her about history and technology. These conversations gave me a very unique perspective on just how much the world has changed. She marveled at automobiles, air travel and even lived to see fax machines and computers. She was impressed with just how far mankind had come during her day. Now, I think to my days as a child. The use of computers in schools only came to be prevalent once I was leaving high school. Video games to play on your TV came a few years later and then a decade later here come fax machines, and I was amazed when I could call a records office and they could fax me the information the same day and not have to be the standard records request by mail and then wait a couple of weeks to get a response and hard copy in the mail. Then along come bulletin boards, email and eventually the Internet.

Those of you closely familiar with my background know I literally have hundreds of Internet patents and Technology patents, so needless to say, I know the power of technology. When I became in tune and familiar with the Internet and what it would eventually become, I knew it would change the world as we knew it. Back then, I was excited about just being able to see text on a computer screen that someone else wrote. In fact, when I first become involved in technology, there were **NO** pictures on the Internet, no web browsers, no music and it was a rip roaring speed of 2800 baud (for you of those who don't know, compared to today's broadband, G4 or G5 and other new technologies)

46

that was the blinding speed equivalent of my 103 year old grandmother trying to outrun a fighter jet. There just is no comparison – at all!

Today we literally have the world of information at our fingertips and even powerful countries such as China, Korea, Iraq and Iran cannot keep outside information away from the common populace. The Internet is too big, too free and too powerful to contain or control. No more Dark Ages, where the Church tells you what to think or say. No more learning only the government approved or ruling party version of a story or subject. It is now all wide open for anyone who wants to know. Even the modern news business, TV and print media alike, are almost and I stress **ALMOST** no longer able to contain or spin stories to their own will and sensationalism. Now, with the advent of the Internet, we are getting closer to a revolution of Pure Truth.

I truly believe and stress to my children, now is an amazing time to live in. No, we are not making mad dashes of exploration to jungles or the Poles, as was recent centuries past, but we are now poised to both **REWRITE** and **CORRECT** history and get the message to the entire world. All of this is directly a result of technology being put in the hands of everyone!

So how does this relate to Treasure Hunting? Not too long ago, someone wanting to do research into a long lost treasure would have to visit libraries (several of them since different libraries would carry different books and reference libraries), travel to tax and records offices and send tons of letters requesting information and hope, just hope you got a response, that sometimes only came a month or even, many months later if you were lucky.

Now – as an absolute truth, "Ask and You Shall Receive", all thanks to the Internet.

Since research is 90% of the success of a treasure hunt, and now you have books, public records, military records and every book ever published at your fingertips, you are a master at research and thus can be a master at Treasure Research, and thus Treasure Hunting.

It **IS** as simple as **"FILL IN THE BLANKS AND FIND YOUR FORTUNE"**.

This book series is all about the research process. In this state by state book series is treasure of every single type. Hidden Hoards, Caches, Stolen Loot, Lost Mines and Forgotten Fortunes, they are all in between these covers. Whether your favorite type of treasure is in Ghost Towns, buried vaults, in desert sands, in mountain hideaways or at the bottom of the seas, there is treasure here for you to find. All you have to do is fill in the blanks.

Some of the stories inside are loaded with such great facts and clues that all someone has to do is load up in their car, get out at the location with a shovel and dig. Other stories in this book will take research work, some more than others and even better, some of the stories in my various books are **TOTAL** misdirection (only four of them in all my books so don't worry about them being too many of them). Why would

I include total horse hockey in any of my books? So you can learn to tell the difference, as the saying goes, "between poop and shoe polish." Kind of hard I know, I am that way. Why would anyone, truly interested in finding lost treasure want fluff and puff? Fluff and Puff is for certain kinds of movies and has no business in the profession of, or for that matter, the recreation of; treasure hunting. Only the hard core facts will pay out.

But you do need to be able to tell the difference between writers' story telling gunk and good, provable treasure clues and leads. So, this book has a little of everything allowing you to hone your skills and hopefully make a fortune.

In my passion of research, my formal team research, and in my schools I use a simple rule called 3x3x3 **C.A.C.H.E.** system. The acronym of **C.A.C.H.E.** is the actual formula for being wildly successful at cache hunting and recovery.

C – Consolidate

A – Authenticate/audit

C – Cull

H – History/historical records

E – Explore/expedition

C.A.C.H.E is the key to cache. If you take the time to fully understand and employ the steps of the cache acronym, then you could become very successful and very wealthy. It all begins and ends with you and your efforts.

C IS FOR CONSOLIDATE

Invariably there are many different versions of any given treasure story. It's the old "telephone game" most of us played as children. Put a classroom of kids in the circle. Whisper a simple to remember phrase or story into the ear of the first student and then have them pass it on in secret to the next student; and so on and so on.

By the time the story comes around back to the teacher, the phrase only minimally resembles the original phrase given to the first student. There four reasons for this phenomenon.

1. **Poor listening skills**
2. **Poor translation skills**
3. **Willful maliciousness**
4. **Human nature**

If you grasp why stories change from person to person and can decipher where they went astray, then you are rapidly and intelligently headed down the path to cache recovery success. It is easy to understand poor listening skills. Most people do not really listen to the actual details of a story. Hundreds and thousands of years ago, when stories were only communicated by word of mouth, people tended to get the story accurate and retell it as told to them. It was a source of pride and was an absolute requirement of the storyteller to get facts flawless. In fact, being the culture's or area's storyteller was a true and noble profession.

However, the advent of published works and with the changes in modern society, we have moved storytelling from truth and accurateness to sensationalism, errors, omissions, and bending the truth to suit one's needs.

Poor translation skills not only mean being unable to retell the story as originally told, it also relates to the literal mistranslation of words between cultures and races of people. Such as the common mistranslation of the meaning of the word "church" as it applies to the Bible. For example:

The English word "church" has various meanings. Webster gives the following definitions for the word church.

1.   a building for public Christian worship.
2.   a religious service in such a building.
3.   (sometimes cap.)

    A.   *the world body of Christian believers; Christendom.*
    B. *any major division of his body; a Christian denomination.*

4.   a Christian congregation.
5.   organized religion as distinguished from the state.
6.   (cap)

    A.   *The Christian church before the Reformation.*
    B. *the Roman Catholic Church.*

7.   the profession of an ecclesiastic -V. C.
8.   to perform a church service of thanksgiving for (a woman after child birth). [Go RI (a)on (DOA) the Lord's house).

Today the word church has a wide variety of meanings from referring to a building to performing a religion service. Although we have an understanding the modern use of the word, it is of more significance in understanding the use of the word in the New Testament. It is essential that we understand its original meaning as it was used in New Testament times.

In our English Bible the Greek word, "ekklesia" is translated in most places "church." The word "ekklesia" is found in one hundred and fifteen places in the New Testament. It is translated in English one hundred and thirteen times "church" and the remaining times it is translated "assembly." In classical Greek the word "ekklesia" meant "an assembly of citizens summoned by the crier, the legislative assembly." The word as used in the New Testament is taken from the root of this word, which simply means to "call out." In New Testament times the word was exclusively used to represent a group of people assembled together for a particular cause or purpose. It was never used exclusively to refer to a "religious meeting or group on a building"

An examination of the Greek word "ekklesia" reveals that the word is properly translated into English as the "assembly" or "congregation." It is used to refer to a group of persons that are organized together for a common purpose and who meet together, and was used as early as the 5th Century B.C.

So the word as originally written, shared, and spoken meant one thing, and today we have other completely different meanings. Case in point: there was a time your gay friends meant those who were "happy," not those in "same sex" relationships. So understanding that poor translations skills always come into play is part of the **C.A.C.H.E.** equation.

Now here comes the can of worms, willful maliciousness, and funny how it follows my comments on the church, since one of the most egregious offenders of this in historical terms and culture terms is the institution of the Church. Throughout history (there is that word again history) stories have been modified, augmented, and embellished to reflect favorably on the ruling class, which in most cases was the Church. Now, remember earlier when I mentioned that there is a practice among treasure lore and lost mine writers to willfully omit facts, leads, elements of case and point to hide the actual facts that made lead to a caches discovery? Well, this is most common fact of interference of man when it comes to cache history and lore. Most of the stories get willingly perverted and the truth compromised.

This point, now naturally leads us to the nature of Mankind. Man, whether in his DNA or his soul tends to embellish for various reasons, i.e. **(a)** deception, **(b)** personal gain, **(c)** entertainment, **(d)** self-preservation, or; **(e)** self-importance or ego. Let's face it. Most people love attention, love being the center of attention, the topic of the story, and the ironically enough, the bearer of bad news.

Bearer of bad news? Who likes to be the bearer of bad news? Well, think about it. All adventurers and explores are commonly sent off by people who relish telling them **(1)** they are fools, **(2)** chasing a dream,

(3) wasting their lives, **(4)** will die in the process, and **(5)** will find nothing! Read any account of famous expeditions. This is just a fact of life and the nature of mankind. Most want to be "The Winners" but do not want others "to," win." You have those people in your life right now and I bet you can easily identify them – the dream killers, the moaners and the "you-can't-do-that" crowd. If you have trouble identifying them in your life, announce you are going on a treasure hunt and stand back and watch their individual responses to your announcements. You know these types of people, and they will always reveal themselves!

So how does all of this relate to **CONSOLIDATE**? The first step in mastering **C.A.C.H.E.** is to consolidate everything you can find published, written, noted, and said about the particular cache you are interested in tracking down. This may be 10 items or a thousand items, but consolidate it all in one central place where you can read, reread, research, and study over and over again. Then, with your understanding of the four historical story and legend phenomena, i.e.

1. **Poor listening skills**
2. **Poor translation skills**
3. **Willful maliciousness**
4. **Human nature**

Start shifting through your information so you can get to the **A** in the **C.A.C.H.E.** formula.

A IS FOR AUTHENTICATE

Authenticate, as defined by the Merriam-Webster Dictionary is a transitive verb: to prove or serve to prove the authenticity of (authenticate a document).

This is the most important step up to this point. Of all the materials, documents, stories, versions of stories, magazine articles, newspaper clippings, and/or firsthand accounts; you must take steps to determine which of them are authentic. For me, I sometimes make a personal columned grid where I lay out the common threads between each of the versions of the story told. When you lay out the details in a grid and look at them as various points of facts, and they are not crowded and drowned in a sea of letters and words, but presented as bullet points, you can start to recognize patterns. This is one of the very same steps a forensic researcher or F. B. I. profiler starts to create a "description or identity" of a serial killer. The various facts, when arranged properly, can reveal clues; important clues that can be easily overlooked.

But at the very same time you are revealing hidden clues, you are also discriminating fact from fiction. You will be able to identify fancy story telling from factual events that will actually lead to the recovery of the cache. Also during this process you are able to identify the subtle changes over time, writer after writer, story teller after story teller; and be able to discern whether something has been either repeated as true or omitted for one reason or another. If you arrange your **CONSOLIDATION** work and sort them during your **AUTHENTICATION** process chronologically, then you are afforded one more edge: history (which will play a huge role later on as you will read). Comparing stories told or retold by chronological dates, allows you to work your way back to the original source; and the closer to the source the more reliable the information. Remember, detectives don't want to interview the friend of a friend who had a friend that saw the crime occur; they want to get to either the dying victims account or the first person witness accounts. And so do you when it comes to Cacheology. Why? So you can begin the next step in the process, **CULL**.

C IS FOR CULL

Here is another transitive verb from Merriam-Webster.
CULL:

1. to select from a group; choose (culled the best passages from the poet's work)
2. to reduce or control the size of (as a herd) by removal (as by hunting) of especially weaker animals; also to hunt or kill (animals) as a means of population control.

Cull, crudely put, is a means of **"CRAP"** control. You need to weigh through the fanciful fabrications and cut to the chase to glean the information that will actually allow you to find the cache. Do not waste your time with useless facts or just decide to pursue a cache hunt with only one story or very little facts. You need fact after verifiable fact. My Professional rule of thumb in going after a particular cache is: three different stories, three different geological anchors, and three verifiable historical accounts or record sources proving the three stories, sources, and individuals involved.

56

Yes, **3x3x3;** it's my matrix formula of verification and begins the culling process. To give you an example of each: If a particular lost mine story has a particular individual's name attached to it, then verify the existence of the individual. If they found the mine and then somewhere along the way they were killed but told no one about the mine, then there may very well exist a mining claim at the claims office. If it was a huge find of gold and the individual needed sources, tools, and funds to mine the claim, then there will more than likely be an assay record and partnership record and that can verify various points.

If the story of the fantastic claim was written about in the local paper, do a few things: (1) check the papers story against the legend, and (2) check the newspaper writers past stories on the topic. Why the second? Was the newspaper man a "fact reporter" or the papers "fanciful writer"? The first lends more credence to the story, the second means you have to find other sources and not trust this newspaperman's account.

Don't get upset or discouraged if you throw out 80% or more of your collected stories on the cache. That's normal and in fact culling more is normal. Use my proven 3x3x3 method of verifying and culling and you too could be a successful cache hunter. If you do you will make history (there is that word again).

H IS FOR HISTORY

History & Historical

Hearsay & Headaches

Hard Work & Head Work

Hysterical & Heartache

Hard fought & Happiness

Each they hunt, hand in hand

The words above have a connection. Each positive begets a positive. Conversely, each negative begets a negative. It is all in how you approach your cache mindset. History is the single most important factor in validating, pinpointing, and recovering a particular cache. If you have history on your side then it is almost as good as having a time machine that will take you back to the very moment in time the cache was deposited.

Whether or not a person means to, they do leave their stamp somewhere along the historical record: censuses, military records, property ownership, shipping manifest and passenger lists. Somewhere the information you seek exists. Searching property records, death and tax records, and information at the local library can go a long way to validating your leads and facts about a certain cache.

If you can go to historic sources and verify the story or lead, and if you can put it into historical context, i.e. three days journey in the 1800s would have been up to a **MAX** of 60 miles, whereby in more recent times, you could have traveled across the whole of the US by car in three days' time. Historical context is paramount. I learned the historical context point the hard way one time when I was looking for an old miner's cabin. I looked and looked for a log cabin but could not find one, and the only broken down wooden structure was a corral. However, the stone miner's cabin was easily found when I corrected for the historical context and location context. A simple change made all the difference in the world.

Adjust your clues according to **HISTORY** and **HISTORICAL CONTEXT** and save yourself a lot of false starts and dead ends.

Now, when reading the stories in this book, please keep in mind the **C.A.C.H.E.** method of detection and validation and see how many clues you can pick out from the stories told and then turn the stories told herein into your very own personal Treasure Case Files.

Now the

E IS FOR EXPLORE

so let's get exploring!

CHAPTER SEVEN

HOW TO BUILD YOUR PERSONAL TREASURE CASE FILES

The difference between a treasure story and a treasure case file is the case file has the relevant clues notated, researched, plotted and ready to put to work for the treasure hunter or Cacheologist.

There are certain things that make a case file a real case file. First, of course, is to stick to the 3x3x3: **<u>3 Different Sources</u>** for the same story, from 3 different geological anchors or perspectives with 3 at least three verifiable individuals who were involved in the same treasure story

Now most people ask, "What are the all elements to the 3x3x3 process?" One, there is **NO WAY** to list all the individual elements needed to verify, cross check and re-verify, but there is a starting point. Besides, as any good researcher knows, the more one investigates, the more clues are found that require further investigation. So, you start with the basics and from there the treasure verification matrix expands, up and until the point you have more than enough information to find what you are looking for, and then you have to get off your duff and go out and get it!

As you read the stories inside, you will notice the following check list or table at the end of each treasure story:

```
Who:_____

What:_____

Where:_____

How:_____

Others:_____

Records/Relatives:_____

Tax/Death/Military:_____

Newspapers:_____

        Internet:_____

        Sources:_____

COMMENTS:_____
_____
_____
_____
_____
_____
_____
_____
```

It is this checklist that will enable you to transform these stories into your very own, highly personalized, Treasure Case Files. You might find you want to go research several treasures at once or you may read this book and just select one that meets your personal criteria and likes. From there, you begin the process of making the case file and as with all good detective or forensic research work, you begin with the **WHO**, **WHAT**, **WHERE**, **WHEN** and **HOW**.

In journalism, the **Five Ws** (also known as the Five Ws (and one H), or Six Ws) is a concept in news style, research, and in police investigations that are regarded as basics in information-gathering. It is a formula for getting the "full" story on something. The maxim of the Five Ws (and one H) is that for a report to be considered complete it must answer a checklist of six questions, each of which comprises an interrogative word:

Who? *Who was involved?*

What? *What happened (what's the story)?*

Where? *Where did it take place?*

When? *When did it take place?*

Why? *Why did it happen?*

How? *How did it happen?*

These principles, as with Journalism, Detective work or any forensic research work, also apply to the research work needed to verify, authenticate and locate lost treasures. The principle underlying the maxim is that each question should elicit a factual answer, thus facts necessary to include for a report to be considered complete. Importantly, none of these questions can be answered with a simple "yes" or "no".

Simple yes or no answers, as with any forensic research, does not **VERIFY** or validate any clues for you to follow to find your treasure. You need facts and as many facts as possible. But, the **WHO**, **WHAT**, **WHERE**, **WHEN**, **WHY** and **HOW** only answer a few of the questions needed to discover the location of a lost treasure. You need to know more. You need to create a map of times, places, people and things, but most important you need to know these facts are reliable. That brings us to the other basic treasure case file questions that need to be asked. On your checklist at the end of each story we have included **OTHERS**.

OTHERS — why others? Simply put, **IF** there were **OTHERS** (additional people involved in the treasure story) then you need to answer the basic questions about all the parties or players involved. When researching one person's background you may come to dead end leads, but when you research everyone involved, it **MOST LIKELY** will give you answers about other people as well and new contacts and links to research out. Simply put, other people involved may give up more clues than the single main player. So **OTHERS** are there to remind you to fully research **ALL** involved and ask yourself "Who else?"

The next items listed are:

RECORDS - RELATIVES - TAX - DEATH - MILITARY

These are self-explanatory, but they are reminders of where to look for additional verification and validation information. Are there shipment records? Did they have relatives in the area? Surviving relatives? Death records? Ancestry Records? Did they serve in the Military? The comprehensive search of these types of records, which are available online, will help you find out more about the players and the **OTHERS** and can actually lead to more **OTHERS**. Remember, when it comes to treasure hunting, the more people involved, the more chance of finding clues and leads.

Next on your story checklist comes:

NEWSPAPERS and **WHAT**

In the beginning of this book I talked about how important using the Internet for research is, but when it comes to Newspapers and the articles and stories of the past, most are on the Internet, just not searchable by the Internet standards. That means, you can't just type in words and hope to find old newspaper stories. Most of the old newspaper stories from the 1700's and 1800's are only scanned in as images, and that means the Internet cannot search for the words in them, so when you do a basic search on the Net, you miss most of the newspaper stories. So the **NEWSPAPERS** section is here to remind you to search the areas **NEWSPAPER**. If it happened in Mesa, Arizona then search the Mesa, Arizona Newspaper via various Newspaper Archives. Once you have logged into the archive, then you can search their system remotely and find what you need. Basically as weird as it sounds it's available over the Net but not on the Net. It's on the Newspaper Archive Files.

And that leads to another **WHAT**, simply meaning **IF** you found a newspaper archive story, **WHAT did it say?** Compare it to the other information you collected.

While searching for a $10 Billion, yes, $10 Billion Dollar lost treasure, I read many books written on the topic and tons of accounts, but it was one rare, very rare newspaper article from 1946 that quoted word for word an article from 1810 that gave me the new and valuable information I needed to find the treasures clues.

INTERNET and **SOURCES** is there to remind you to write down and digitally store your Internet Sources for your fact finding. The Internet grows daily and servers go down and websites go out of business hourly. Don't just think you can remember the website you found the information from, chances are you cannot. The volume of information is much too great. So **LOG** your Internet sites and your sources. This means the **WHOLE** web address and not just a name of a website. Again the pages of a web site grow daily and thus pages change daily and server space is made daily by discarding old files. Those files just may be the old story you thought you could go back to.

As a rule of thumb, I do the following on Internet Based sources:

1. **ADD** the **LINK** to your Favorites file in your Web Browser
2. **PRINT** a **HARD COPY** of the information for your hard files
3. **SAVE** a **MIRROR COPY** of the websites pages containing the information you needed and store this to your hard drive. There are many software programs that can mirror image a web page for your computer.
4. **BACK UP! BACK UP! BACK UP ALL YOUR FILES!**

And finally, I have added a **COMMENTS** section so you can add comments on a treasure story as you are inspired and don't lose it by trying to remember to notate it later

READ THIS BOOK WITH A PEN IN HAND!! GO AHEAD AND GET ONE, I WILL WAIT!

And since most people need to be told three times to remember something, well so, here you are. Are you willing to fill in the blanks?

The only thing standing between you and a fortune in lost gold is **RESEARCH.**

If you are willing to fill in the blanks, you can fill your pockets with a fortune.

Got something to write with?

Then let's get going!

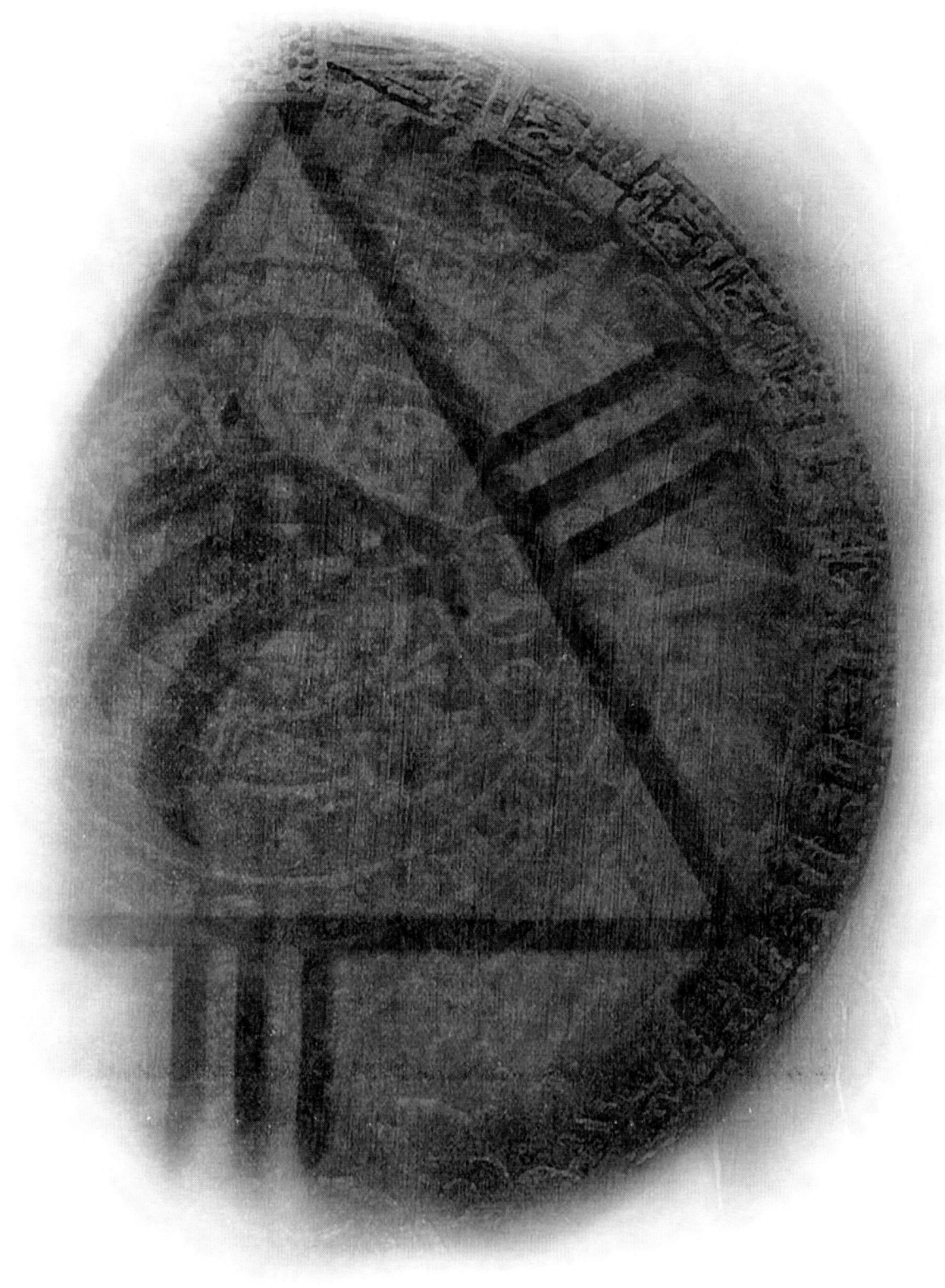

CHAPTER EIGHT

ARIZONA

THE LOST DUTCHMAN'S MINE

THE LOST DUTCHMAN'S MINE

In the 1840s, three prospectors known as the Peralta brothers stumbled upon a mine full of gold in the Superstition Mountains of Arizona, sixty miles east of Phoenix. Located on 160,000 acres in Apache Junction, the mine was said to have eight veins of gold ore. After lugging as much gold as they could carry back to their village, they returned with more than a hundred others and mules to help transport the loot. In 1848, the Apache Indians, one of several tribes native to the area, became furious that their sacred mountain was being plundered and disgraced. They launched a surprise attack on the large entourage and many of the villagers, including two of the Peralta brothers, were killed. The Indian women promptly covered and hid the gold with dirt to protect the mine from more outsiders.

To his delight, survivor Ramon Peralta (one of the original threesome) and two other friends rediscovered the mine in the 1870s. Soon after, they met a German man named Jacob Waltz who was becoming a well known prospector. He had immigrated to the United States in 1839 while he was in his late twenties, with dreams of striking gold and becoming rich. He lived and dug for gold in North Carolina, followed by Georgia, and then Mississippi. He was not successful. He then tried his hand at mining for gold in California, and stuck with it for eleven years. With no results for all his labors, he departed with a group for the Bradshaw Mountains of Arizona, hoping to finally realize his dream. It was in these mountains of Arizona that he met Ramon who told him about the secret mine of gold in the Superstition Mountains.

Unfortunately, that mistake cost Ramon his life. Jacob greedily killed Ramon and his comrades and was then the only person left who knew the location of the mine, other than the Apaches. From that moment until his death in 1891, he never told anyone the location and was able to secretly travel back and forth to the treasure each year without being followed, or noticed.

While on his deathbed, he wrote out directions and a map for his close confidante, Julia Thomas, and a German friend. He told them the gold was worth $100 million. After three months of searching, they turned up empty-handed. Over the next hundred years, many groups and individuals have attempted to locate the secret mine and have been unsuccessful. The Phelps-Dodge Corporation financed a thorough hunt for the mine with experienced prospectors and geologists, but to no avail. There is a theory that the mine may have capsized during an 1877 earthquake.

However, in 1914, $18,000 worth of gold ore was discovered in the exact spot where the Apache attack had occurred. Overall, more than twenty people have died while searching for the lost mine, giving credibility to the superstition that the Indians laid a curse against all who would try to invade their mountain. Other legends say that the entrance to the mine is guarded by Pygmies, or that an old prospector shoots all who get too close. Over one thousand treasure seekers have scoured the mountain, searching for a glimpse of this enormous fortune. A report was once made stating that to find the mine-one must study the Mexican symbols carved into cliffs within a five-mile radius of El Sombrero Peak. Jacob Waltz also left another secretly coded clue to his friends when he died:

"No miner will find my mine. To find my mine you must pass a cow barn. From my mine you can see the military trail, but from the military trail you cannot see my mine. The rays of the setting sun shine into the entrance of my mine. There is a trick in the trail to my mine. My mine is located in a north-trending canyon. There is a rock face on the trail to my mine."

As recently as the summer of 2009, one man has claimed to have solved the riddle of this Lost Dutchman's Mine. He states,

"I have located the gold. I am John V. Kemm of Albuquerque, New Mexico. The key is the heart: the Peralta map is close to dead on until you reach the heart, then reverse the heart or spin it to the right and a little to the north. From a specific angle from Weaver's needle, you can see the heart's center. The upper left side is where the gold is and this can be verified on Google Earth. All I ask for is credit for the find and, if there are profits made, three percent of the total for me and my family. Again, my name is John V. Kemm, age 43, of Albuquerque, New Mexico. I encourage anyone to investigate this finding of mine."

Who:_____

What:_____

Where:_____

How:_____

Others:_____

Records/Relatives:_____

Tax/Death/Military:_____

Newspapers:_____

Internet:_____

Sources:_____

COMMENTS:_____

_____

_____

_____

_____

_____

_____

_____

_____

_____

Who:_____

What:_____

Where:_____

How:_____

Others:_____

Records/Relatives:_____

Tax/Death/Military:_____

Newspapers:_____

Internet:_____

Sources:_____

COMMENTS:_____

_____

_____

_____

_____

_____

_____

_____

_____

_____

Who:_____

What:_____

Where:_____

How:_____

Others:_____

Records/Relatives:_____

Tax/Death/Military:_____

Newspapers:_____

    Internet:_____

    Sources:_____

COMMENTS:_____

_____

_____

_____

_____

_____

_____

_____

_____

_____

_____

Who:_____

What:_____

Where:_____

How:_____

Others:_____

Records/Relatives:_____

Tax/Death/Military:_____

Newspapers:_____

    Internet:_____

    Sources:_____

COMMENTS:_____

_____

_____

_____

_____

_____

_____

_____

_____

_____

Who:_____

What:_____

Where:_____

How:_____

Others:_____

Records/Relatives:_____

Tax/Death/Military:_____

Newspapers:_____

    Internet:_____

    Sources:_____

COMMENTS:_____

_____

_____

_____

_____

_____

_____

_____

_____

_____

Who:_____

What:_____

Where:_____

How:_____

Others:_____

Records/Relatives:_____

Tax/Death/Military:_____

Newspapers:_____

    Internet:_____

    Sources:_____

COMMENTS:_____

_____

_____

_____

_____

_____

_____

_____

_____

_____

NOTES

NOTES

_____
_____
_____
_____
_____
_____
_____
_____
_____
_____
_____
_____
_____
_____
_____
_____
_____
_____
_____
_____

NOTES

NOTES

_____

_____

_____

_____

_____

_____

_____

_____

_____

_____

_____

_____

_____

_____

_____

_____

_____

_____

_____

_____

_____

NOTES

NOTES

_____

_____

_____

_____

_____

_____

_____

_____

_____

_____

_____

_____

_____

_____

_____

_____

_____

_____

_____

NOTES

NOTES

NOTES

NOTES

_____

_____

_____

_____

_____

_____

_____

_____

_____

_____

_____

_____

_____

_____

_____

_____

_____

_____

_____

CHAPTER NINE

ARIZONA

THE LOST MINE OF BRONCO CANYON

THE LOST MINE OF BRONCO CANYON

A legend has been passed down for generations concerning the small town of Bumble Bee, Arizona and nearby Bronco Canyon. It is believed that a large cache of two hundred pounds of raw gold is sitting on the bottom of a creek, near where Slate Creek and Squaw Creek meet. Today, Bumble Bee is a ghost town, completely deserted. Much of the town remains exactly as it looked in the 1800s, save for a few restored buildings which were renovated in preparation of a tourist attraction. The town was purchased in 1960 by newspaper executive Charles King who planned to create an authentic railroad museum and draw in a large market for tourism. His plan never materialized.

How the gold arrived in the creek is a simple story. In the late nineteenth century, two miners, Brown and Davis, had been prospecting in the nearby area and decided to venture into the west side of Bronco Canyon. As they searched, they made a discovery of an 18 inch rich vein of gold quartz. The miners stayed in the canyon and labored each day to remove the gold, which they stored at the bottom of a creek, eight miles away at the intersection of the Slate Creek and Squaw Creek. As autumn passed and a cold winter was imminent, they decided to head home. They packed up a total of twenty-five sacks of gold. As they began on their journey, a gathering of Apache Indians flocked to the canyon and attacked the duo. One of the prospectors was killed and the other desperately escaped amid the din, under a pile of rocks between a large boulder and a stratum of white volcanic ash that outcropped along the foot of the mountains on the east side of the canyon, left Davis' pick stabbed into the quartz vein to mark the location, and escaped out of the canyon after nightfall only taking as much gold with him as he could carry. The survivor headed home with an incredible story and the hopes of reuniting with his gold in the future. Desiring to wait until the area was calm and Indian-free; the memories of his find had to suffice.

Years passed and the Indians were no longer a threat in the area, yet the miner was too old and weak to make the journey. As he lay on his deathbed, he disclosed the location of the vein and the hidden sacks of gold. He estimated the value of the twenty-five bags to be worth $80,000 at the time.

Many years later, a Mexican shepherd noticed a rusty pick stuck in a quartz outcropping, but was unaware of the presence of gold in the vicinity and therefore did not launch a search. Other explorers have attempted to search the creek bed for the two hundred pounds, near the canyon for the stashed loot, and the canyon itself for the rich vein. None of the three has ever been found.

Bumble Bee is located in Yavapai County, New Mexico, in Bronco Canyon, just north of Black Canyon. It is eight miles south of Cordes. The two creeks intersect about four miles east of Bumble Bee. The $80,000 in gold ore today would be worth an amazing $5,000,000!

Who:_____

What:_____

Where:_____

How:_____

Others:_____

Records/Relatives:_____

Tax/Death/Military:_____

Newspapers:_____

    Internet:_____

    Sources:_____

COMMENTS:_____

_____

_____

_____

_____

_____

_____

_____

_____

_____

Who:_____

What:_____

Where:_____

How:_____

Others:_____

Records/Relatives:_____

Tax/Death/Military:_____

Newspapers:_____

    Internet:_____

    Sources:_____

COMMENTS:_____

_____

_____

_____

_____

_____

_____

_____

_____

_____

Who:_____

What:_____

Where:_____

How:_____

Others:_____

Records/Relatives:_____

Tax/Death/Military:_____

Newspapers:_____

    Internet:_____

    Sources:_____

COMMENTS:_____

_____

_____

_____

_____

_____

_____

_____

_____

_____

_____

Who:_____

What:_____

Where:_____

How:_____

Others:_____

Records/Relatives:_____

Tax/Death/Military:_____

Newspapers:_____

    Internet:_____

    Sources:_____

COMMENTS:_____

_____

_____

_____

_____

_____

_____

_____

_____

_____

Who:_____

What:_____

Where:_____

How:_____

Others:_____

Records/Relatives:_____

Tax/Death/Military:_____

Newspapers:_____

    Internet:_____

    Sources:_____

COMMENTS:_____

_____

_____

_____

_____

_____

_____

_____

_____

_____

_____

Who:_____

What:_____

Where:_____

How:_____

Others:_____

Records/Relatives:_____

Tax/Death/Military:_____

Newspapers:_____

    Internet:_____

    Sources:_____

COMMENTS:_____

_____

_____

_____

_____

_____

_____

_____

_____

_____

NOTES

_____
_____
_____
_____
_____
_____
_____
_____
_____
_____
_____
_____
_____
_____
_____
_____
_____
_____
_____
_____

NOTES

NOTES

NOTES

_____
_____
_____
_____
_____
_____
_____
_____
_____
_____
_____
_____
_____
_____
_____
_____
_____
_____
_____

NOTES

NOTES

NOTES

_____

_____

_____

_____

_____

_____

_____

_____

_____

_____

_____

_____

_____

_____

_____

_____

_____

_____

_____

_____

NOTES

_____

_____

_____

_____

_____

_____

_____

_____

_____

_____

_____

_____

_____

_____

_____

_____

_____

_____

_____

_____

NOTES

_____

_____

_____

_____

_____

_____

_____

_____

_____

_____

_____

_____

_____

_____

_____

_____

_____

_____

_____

_____

_____

_____

NOTES

CHAPTER TEN

ARIZONA

THE LOST CITY AND TREASURE OF THE GRAND CANYON

THE LOST CITY AND TREASURE OF THE GRAND CANYON

Towards the beginning of the twentieth century, stories began floating around the southwestern region of America concerning the remnants of a lost Egyptian city found at the northern end of the Grand Canyon. An explorer had found the entrance to these cities through a hidden cave while journeying along the Colorado River.

The Arizona Gazette published an article on April 5, 1909 describing his discovery. The article detailed the hidden citadel discovered by G.E. Kincaid, who was convinced that the former inhabitants were of Egyptian race. He gave descriptions of mummies, idols, and a large shrine to Buddha. Everything in the underground world was incredibly well preserved and the formerly occupied system of tunnels and caves could have housed more than 50,000 people. Interested in this hypothesis, historian and linguist Carl Hart, editor of Word Explorer, obtained a hiker's map of the Grand Canyon from a bookstore in Chicago. Analyzing the map, he noticed that much of the area on the north side of the canyon has Egyptian names. The area around Ninety-Four Mile Creek and Trinity Creek contains rock formations with names like Tower of Set, Tower of Ra, Horus Temple, Osiris Temple, and Isis Temple.

The Gazette article interviewed two people from the Smithsonian Institution: G. E Kincaid and Professor S. A. Jordan. The 1909 article clearly states that the Smithsonian is involved with studying and excavating the site. However, the Smithsonian denies that any such discovery ever occurred. This brings up the larger question that if this was a true story, why would the Smithsonian have covered up what certainly would be one of the most significant archeological finds of the twentieth century? Believe it or not, there is precedence for the Smithsonian losing information about discoveries that are deemed to not fit in with currently accepted dogma about the history of America and its interaction or lack thereof with other ancient civilizations.

The article begins: "The latest news of the progress of the explorations of what is now regarded by scientists as not only the oldest archaeological discovery in the United States, but one of the most valuable in the world, which was mentioned some time ago in the Gazette." A month earlier, the Gazette printed an article mentioning Kincaid's exploration, stating that he was unearthing some major archaeological discoveries to be confirmed at a later date.

The original, briefer article from March 12 explains that Kincaid traveled the entire length of the Colorado River by wooden boat and that there was only one man who had accomplished this feat before. It was John Wesley Powell who explored the Colorado River and the Grand Canyon from 1869 to 1872.

In his book Exploration of the Colorado River and its Canyons, Powell describes his journey through the Grand Canyon. While passing through an area known as Marble Canyon, Powell noticed in the canyon walls great numbers of caves that were hollowed out. Also communicated from Kincaid's report to the Gazette in April were several descriptions of what he had found. Several hundred rooms were discovered, reached by passageways running from the main passage, one of them having been explored for 854 feet and another 634 feet. War weapons, copper instruments, sharp-edged and hard as steel, indicate the high state of civilization reached by these strange people. Years later, Kincaid related a very detailed description of his discovery:

"First, I would impress that the cavern is nearly inaccessible. The entrance is 1,486 feet down the sheer canyon wall. It is located on government land and no visitor will be allowed there under penalty of trespass. The scientists wish to work unmolested, without fear of archeological discoveries being disturbed by curio or relic hunters. A trip there would be fruitless, and the visitor would be sent on his way. The story of how I found the cavern has been related, but in a paragraph: I was journeying down the Colorado River in a boat, alone, looking for mineral. Some forty-two miles up the river from the El Tovar Crystal canyon, I saw on the east wall, stains in the sedimentary formation about 2,000 feet above the river bed. There was no trail to this point, but I finally reached it with great difficulty.

"Above a shelf which hid it from view from the river, was the mouth of the cave. There are steps leading from this entrance some thirty yards to what was, at the time the cavern was inhabited, the level of the river. When I saw the chisel marks on the wall inside the entrance, I became interested, securing my gun and went in. During that trip I went back several hundred feet along the main passage till I came to the crypt in which I discovered the mummies. One of these I stood up and photographed by flashlight. I gathered a number of relics, which I carried down the Colorado to Yuma, from whence I shipped them to Washington with details of the discovery. Following this, government explorations were undertaken.

"The main passageway is about 12 feet wide, narrowing to nine feet toward the farther end. About 57 feet from the entrance, the first side-passages branch off to the right and left, along which, on both sides, are a number of rooms about the size of ordinary living rooms of today, though some are 30 by 40 feet square. These are entered by oval-shaped doors and are ventilated by round air spaces through the walls into the passages. The walls are about three feet six inches in thickness.

"The passages are chiseled or hewn as straight as could be laid out by an engineer. The ceilings of many of the rooms converge to a center. The side-passages near the entrance run at a sharp angle from the main hall, but toward the rear they gradually reach a right angle in direction. A gray metal is also found in this cavern, which puzzles the scientists, for its identity has not been established. It resembles platinum."

In his book Lost Cities of North and Central America, David Hatcher Childress discusses this lost city and shares an interesting theory that the Grand Canyon may be the site of the famed King Solomon Mines. Later on, in 1912, the New York Times printed a front page article with the title: "Tell of Vast Riches in the Grand Canyon... Men Engaged in Gold Dredging Operations Expect to Astonish the World." F.D. Watson, the director on the ground overseeing the entire recovery stated, "Exposed to sight are billions of yards of gold-filled silt, containing more billions in dollars in wealth of precious metal than the human mind can possibly grasp in computation. For two years we have been experimenting on methods of extracting and saving the gold and other metals." Watson pulled himself away from Lee's Ferry for a short time to plan for future arrangements and give an update on the status of the recovery; declaring that when the whole field had been developed, the supply of gold in the world will have been increased by billions. "I know that it will be difficult to comprehend that I have a correct conception of the wealth that is buried in the banks of the canyon, but I can demonstrate every statement I make to be absolutely true, and that my chief shortcoming is an inability to comprehend the vastness of the riches that lie along that great stream."

Who:_____

What:_____

Where:_____

How:_____

Others:_____

Records/Relatives:_____

Tax/Death/Military:_____

Newspapers:_____

    Internet:_____

    Sources:_____

COMMENTS:_____

_____

_____

_____

_____

_____

_____

_____

_____

_____

Who:_____

What:_____

Where:_____

How:_____

Others:_____

Records/Relatives:_____

Tax/Death/Military:_____

Newspapers:_____

    Internet:_____

    Sources:_____

COMMENTS:_____

_____

_____

_____

_____

_____

_____

_____

_____

_____

Who:_____

What:_____

Where:_____

How:_____

Others:_____

Records/Relatives:_____

Tax/Death/Military:_____

Newspapers:_____

　　Internet:_____

　　Sources:_____

COMMENTS:_____

_____

_____

_____

_____

_____

_____

_____

_____

_____

Who:_____

What:_____

Where:_____

How:_____

Others:_____

Records/Relatives:_____

Tax/Death/Military:_____

Newspapers:_____

    Internet:_____

    Sources:_____

COMMENTS:_____

_____

_____

_____

_____

_____

_____

_____

_____

_____

Who:_____

What:_____

Where:_____

How:_____

Others:_____

Records/Relatives:_____

Tax/Death/Military:_____

Newspapers:_____

    Internet:_____

    Sources:_____

COMMENTS:_____

_____

_____

_____

_____

_____

_____

_____

_____

_____

Who:_____

What:_____

Where:_____

How:_____

Others:_____

Records/Relatives:_____

Tax/Death/Military:_____

Newspapers:_____

    Internet:_____

    Sources:_____

COMMENTS:_____

_____

_____

_____

_____

_____

_____

_____

_____

_____

NOTES

_____

_____

_____

_____

_____

_____

_____

_____

_____

_____

_____

_____

_____

_____

_____

_____

_____

_____

_____

_____

_____

NOTES

NOTES

NOTES

_____

_____

_____

_____

_____

_____

_____

_____

_____

_____

_____

_____

_____

_____

_____

_____

_____

_____

_____

_____

_____

NOTES

NOTES

NOTES

NOTES

_____

_____

_____

_____

_____

_____

_____

_____

_____

_____

_____

_____

_____

_____

_____

_____

_____

_____

_____

_____

_____

NOTES

NOTES

CHAPTER ELEVEN

ARIZONA

THE PEGLEG MINE

THE PEGLEG MINE

One of the most sought after "lost" mines in the country is Pegleg's Mine, in the Chocolate Mountains of Arizona. Thomas L. "Pegleg" Smith, who lived in the early to middle nineteenth century, was a mountain man who, while serving as a guide for many early expeditions into the American Southwest, helped explore parts of present-day New Mexico. He is also known as a fur trapper, prospector, and horse thief. He lost his leg to an arrow during a trapping expedition in the fall of 1827. After his leg was amputated, his friends fashioned him a wooden leg, thus earning him the name Pegleg.

In the late 1820s, his current expedition had obtained many pelts and decided to take them to Los Angeles for a quick sale. Pegleg and one companion were chosen to make the trip through the desert. As they traveled, Pegleg collected some small rocks from on top of a butte in the Colorado Desert. The butte was one of three in the same general area. Thinking they were copper, he added them to his pack and continued on the journey.

In Los Angeles, he received an appraisal that the small rocks were actually gold. While there, he became intoxicated, started a brawl in the local saloon, and was quickly kicked out of town by the authorities. As he made his way out of California, he stole 300 horses and herded them to Taos, New Mexico to sell for profit.

Eventually, in the 1840s, Pegleg settled down from his crime spree and started a trading post along the Oregon Trail in Idaho, specializing in the sale of horses.

It wasn't until after the 1849 Gold Rush that Pegleg returned to California to organize assistance in his expedition to locate the butte where he found the black gold nuggets. As his expeditions wandered around the desert with no sign of the site, Pegleg ended up deserting the group and heading back to Los Angeles.

In 1853, Pegleg recruited a second mission to locate the gold which also proved to be a failure. Eventually, a third expedition was launched to search for a different lost mine near the Virgin River, where a fellow trap-per, Dutch George Yount, claimed he discovered a ledge full of gold. This journey left him empty-handed as well.

There are those who claimed to have found Pegleg's Lost Mine. One story recounts the travels of a discharged soldier who followed Pegleg's trail from Yuma to Los Angeles. While traveling through the desert, he discovered the three buttes described in Pegleg's account and also found gold nuggets. After arriving in Los Angeles, he showed his friends the nuggets and planned a return trip with professionals to head to the desert and mine the gold. This soldier and his expedition never made it to the Chocolate Mountains and instead were found dead near the base of the San Ysidro Mountains in California.

There are three Indian legends of black-coated gold in the desert that support the existence of Pegleg's mine. The Apache Indians spoke of a place in the desert where the ground was littered with gold nuggets. It was against the tribal law and beliefs of the Apaches to tell others where the gold was located. To this day, the mysterious Pegleg Mine has never been found.

Who:_____

What:_____

Where:_____

How:_____

Others:_____

Records/Relatives:_____

Tax/Death/Military:_____

Newspapers:_____

    Internet:_____

    Sources:_____

COMMENTS:_____

_____

_____

_____

_____

_____

_____

_____

_____

_____

Who:_____

What:_____

Where:_____

How:_____

Others:_____

Records/Relatives:_____

Tax/Death/Military:_____

Newspapers:_____

    Internet:_____

    Sources:_____

COMMENTS:_____

_____

_____

_____

_____

_____

_____

_____

_____

_____

_____

Who:_____

What:_____

Where:_____

How:_____

Others:_____

Records/Relatives:_____

Tax/Death/Military:_____

Newspapers:_____

    Internet:_____

    Sources:_____

COMMENTS:_____

_____

_____

_____

_____

_____

_____

_____

_____

Who:_____

What:_____

Where:_____

How:_____

Others:_____

Records/Relatives:_____

Tax/Death/Military:_____

Newspapers:_____

    Internet:_____

    Sources:_____

COMMENTS:_____

_____

_____

_____

_____

_____

_____

_____

_____

_____

_____

Who:_____

What:_____

Where:_____

How:_____

Others:_____

Records/Relatives:_____

Tax/Death/Military:_____

Newspapers:_____

    Internet:_____

    Sources:_____

COMMENTS:_____

_____

_____

_____

_____

_____

_____

_____

_____

_____

Who:_____

What:_____

Where:_____

How:_____

Others:_____

Records/Relatives:_____

Tax/Death/Military:_____

Newspapers:_____

    Internet:_____

    Sources:_____

COMMENTS:_____

_____

_____

_____

_____

_____

_____

_____

_____

_____

NOTES

_____

_____

_____

_____

_____

_____

_____

_____

_____

_____

_____

_____

_____

_____

_____

_____

_____

_____

_____

_____

NOTES

NOTES

NOTES

NOTES

NOTES

NOTES

_____
_____
_____
_____
_____
_____
_____
_____
_____
_____
_____
_____
_____
_____
_____
_____
_____
_____
_____
_____
_____
_____
_____

NOTES

_____

_____

_____

_____

_____

_____

_____

_____

_____

_____

_____

_____

_____

_____

_____

_____

_____

_____

_____

_____

NOTES

_____

_____

_____

_____

_____

_____

_____

_____

_____

_____

_____

_____

_____

_____

_____

_____

_____

_____

_____

_____

NOTES

CHAPTER TWELVE

ARIZONA

WAGONER'S MINE

WAGONER'S MINE

The Superstition Mountains, located in the desert of Arizona, tower over the horizon a mere thirty-five miles east of Phoenix. They were formerly known as the Salt River Mountains and are located in fierce and rugged country. Weaver's Needle and Miner's Needle, both contained within the Superstition Mountains, are two of the most well-known landscape features in the entire state. Weaver's Needle is a skinny rock face that extends over the mountain summits at the heads of Needle Canyon and East Boulder Canyon. It was named after the famous prospector Paulino Weaver. Miner's Needle is located just three miles southeast of Weaver's Needle, at the head of Whitlow Canyon, and reaches to a height of 3648 feet. Both needles are important landmarks connected to the Lost Dutch-man Mine. Miner's Needle is also associated to at least two other lost gold mines in the area, including the Lost Wagoner Mine.

Wagoner discovered his mine in the late nineteenth century. While residing in the ore milling town of Pinal City, he would process the ore and silver from mines located in Superior, Arizona and other nearby towns. As he witnessed the rich ore that made its way into his mill, he became interested in the idea of prospecting. He began in the mountains surrounding Pinal City, and continued west to the Superstition Mountains.

Wagoner patiently mined everyday in the range, waiting for the big find that he knew would someday happen to him, just as it had to so many others. On one particular day, he was mining on the northern region, near Tortilla Flat, when he was led to follow along La Barge Canyon. He eventually passed Miner's Needle and continued his exploration southward. It was here that his amazing discovery was made – he arrived upon a lode of gold-bearing rose quartz. Overjoyed, Wagoner collected the ore quickly and continued on his southward expedition toward Pinal City. When he entered the town, he sold the ore and congratulated himself for making such a lucrative discovery. Wagoner journeyed back to his secret mine on many occasions, each time accessing the mountain range just north of the Whitlow Ranch, which today is known as Queen Valley. After many years, Wagoner moved away from the Superstition Mountain region, disguising the mine with rocks and debris before his departure. The secret mine of Wagoner has never been found.

Who:_____

What:_____

Where:_____

How:_____

Others:_____

Records/Relatives:_____

Tax/Death/Military:_____

Newspapers:_____

Internet:_____

Sources:_____

COMMENTS:_____

_____

_____

_____

_____

_____

_____

_____

_____

_____

Who:_____

What:_____

Where:_____

How:_____

Others:_____

Records/Relatives:_____

Tax/Death/Military:_____

Newspapers:_____

    Internet:_____

    Sources:_____

COMMENTS:_____

_____

_____

_____

_____

_____

_____

_____

_____

Who:_____

What:_____

Where:_____

How:_____

Others:_____

Records/Relatives:_____

Tax/Death/Military:_____

Newspapers:_____

    Internet:_____

    Sources:_____

COMMENTS:_____

_____

_____

_____

_____

_____

_____

_____

_____

_____

Who:_____

What:_____

Where:_____

How:_____

Others:_____

Records/Relatives:_____

Tax/Death/Military:_____

Newspapers:_____

Internet:_____

Sources:_____

COMMENTS:_____

_____

_____

_____

_____

_____

_____

_____

_____

Who:_____

What:_____

Where:_____

How:_____

Others:_____

Records/Relatives:_____

Tax/Death/Military:_____

Newspapers:_____

    Internet:_____

    Sources:_____

COMMENTS:_____

_____

_____

_____

_____

_____

_____

_____

_____

_____

Who:_____

What:_____

Where:_____

How:_____

Others:_____

Records/Relatives:_____

Tax/Death/Military:_____

Newspapers:_____

    Internet:_____

    Sources:_____

COMMENTS:_____

_____

_____

_____

_____

_____

_____

_____

_____

_____

_____

NOTES

_____

_____

_____

_____

_____

_____

_____

_____

_____

_____

_____

_____

_____

_____

_____

_____

_____

_____

NOTES

NOTES

_____

_____

_____

_____

_____

_____

_____

_____

_____

_____

_____

_____

_____

_____

_____

_____

_____

_____

NOTES

NOTES

_____

_____

_____

_____

_____

_____

_____

_____

_____

_____

_____

_____

_____

_____

_____

_____

_____

_____

_____

_____

_____

_____

NOTES

NOTES

_____
_____
_____
_____
_____
_____
_____
_____
_____
_____
_____
_____
_____
_____
_____
_____
_____
_____

NOTES

NOTES

_____

_____

_____

_____

_____

_____

_____

_____

_____

_____

_____

_____

_____

_____

_____

_____

_____

_____

_____

_____

_____

_____

NOTES

CHAPTER THIRTEEN

ARIZONA

BRONCO BILL'S TREASURE

BRONCO BILL'S TREASURE

In the late nineteenth century, William E. Walters was born in Fort Sill, Oklahoma. His nickname became Bronco Bill. As an adult, he worked as a cowboy and a railroader, but eventually resorted to a bandit lifestyle, joining hands with the Black Jack Ketchum gang in Arizona. He quickly became a pro at taking over railroads and stagecoaches. After shooting various men and robbing them, he decided to start his own gang which would focus on thefts of Wells Fargo stagecoaches.

He recruited several men to join him and they were quick to oblige. He soon became a widely-known criminal, conducting all of his crimes in Arizona and New Mexico. He was listed specifically by Wells Fargo as a public enemy. The bank sent for two no-nonsense lawmen by the names of Jeff Milton and George Scarborough to lead the way in ensuring his swift capture.

After receiving this public enemy status and being assigned two personal bounty hunters, Bronco Bill was soon captured with his gang outside of Solomonville, Arizona in a secret hideout, yet not as secret as he had imagined. One of his gang was killed and Bronco Bill was seriously injured from a gunshot wound. It is near this meeting place where the stolen Wells Fargo riches and gold are said to be buried.

No longer a free man, Bronco Bill was charged and convicted of train robbery. He received a sentence of life in prison. To their horror, Wells Fargo was unable to find and recover the buried gold in the secret hideout. It is believed that the gang leader would never have hidden the loot in an area that would be relatively easy to find. It would have to be nearby the hideout, but not in an obvious place.

In 1917, Bronco Bill was released from prison and sent to Hachita, New Mexico. Hachita was a small, quiet town where Bronco Bill could start his new life under his given name of William Walters. There, he worked as a wrangler at a ranching supply center known as the Diamond A Cattle Company.

He never returned to Solomonville, preferring instead to stay out of trouble and out of prison. He was later killed when he fell from a windmill tower he was repairing. Since he never made it back to the hideout to collect his stash, and he certainly didn't have time to spend it while he was living there, it is widely believed that the Wells Fargo gold is still buried in or around Solomonville, in Graham County, Arizona.

Who:_____

What:_____

Where:_____

How:_____

Others:_____

Records/Relatives:_____

Tax/Death/Military:_____

Newspapers:_____

   Internet:_____

   Sources:_____

COMMENTS:_____

_____

_____

_____

_____

_____

_____

_____

_____

_____

Who:_____

What:_____

Where:_____

How:_____

Others:_____

Records/Relatives:_____

Tax/Death/Military:_____

Newspapers:_____

Internet:_____

Sources:_____

COMMENTS:_____

_____

_____

_____

_____

_____

_____

_____

_____

_____

Who:_____

What:_____

Where:_____

How:_____

Others:_____

Records/Relatives:_____

Tax/Death/Military:_____

Newspapers:_____

    Internet:_____

    Sources:_____

COMMENTS:_____

_____

_____

_____

_____

_____

_____

_____

_____

_____

Who:_____

What:_____

Where:_____

How:_____

Others:_____

Records/Relatives:_____

Tax/Death/Military:_____

Newspapers:_____

Internet:_____

Sources:_____

COMMENTS:_____

_____

_____

_____

_____

_____

_____

_____

_____

_____

Who:_____

What:_____

Where:_____

How:_____

Others:_____

Records/Relatives:_____

Tax/Death/Military:_____

Newspapers:_____

    Internet:_____

    Sources:_____

COMMENTS:_____

_____

_____

_____

_____

_____

_____

_____

_____

_____

Who:_____

What:_____

Where:_____

How:_____

Others:_____

Records/Relatives:_____

Tax/Death/Military:_____

Newspapers:_____

Internet:_____

Sources:_____

COMMENTS:_____

_____

_____

_____

_____

_____

_____

_____

_____

_____

NOTES

_____

_____

_____

_____

_____

_____

_____

_____

_____

_____

_____

_____

_____

_____

_____

_____

_____

_____

_____

_____

_____

_____

_____

_____

NOTES

NOTES

NOTES

_____

_____

_____

_____

_____

_____

_____

_____

_____

_____

_____

_____

_____

_____

_____

_____

_____

_____

_____

_____

_____

_____

NOTES

_____
_____
_____
_____
_____
_____
_____
_____
_____
_____
_____
_____
_____
_____
_____
_____
_____
_____
_____
_____

NOTES

NOTES

_____

_____

_____

_____

_____

_____

_____

_____

_____

_____

_____

_____

_____

_____

_____

_____

_____

_____

_____

NOTES

NOTES

_____

_____

_____

_____

_____

_____

_____

_____

_____

_____

_____

_____

_____

_____

_____

_____

_____

_____

_____

_____

NOTES

CHAPTER FOURTEEN

ARIZONA

THE LOST SPANISH MINE OF SYCAMORE CANYON

THE LOST SPANISH MINE OF SYCAMORE CANYON

In the year 1540, Coronado of Spain journeyed on a personal pilgrimage to the southwestern region of America on a quest for gold. As he traveled through Arizona clear through to Kansas, there was not one ounce of precious metal to be had, at least not for Coronado.

Fast forward forty years. The Spaniards now returned for a second time to continue their fateful search for gold, this time with their guide Antonio de Espejo. Forty years was a short time to wait considering the reputation earned as a result of their earlier expedition, fruitlessly searching the continent. This trip would be different.

The explorers journeyed up the Rio Grande River to a village Tiguex, and from there headed westward, away from the riverbanks. As they encountered the Hopi villages Oraibi, they turned again, heading southwest into the choppy, rough terrain known as the mountains of central Arizona. However breathtaking the views were in this territory full of mountains and canyons alike, the Spaniards would simply not be content without an ore discovery.

Well, it was there, in what is today called Jerome, Arizona, that they caught their first glimpse of precious metals. The ground contained silver and copper deposits, both rich in nature. They quickly realized that the local Indians had been mining some of the oxidized copper ores for paints and pigment. Espejo also uncovered a treasure of sorts, a large mine shaft, hewn out of the rock by the Indians.

But it seemed this silver and copper find was not a dramatic enough find for Espejo's men. They were keenly desirous of the more lucrative gold.

As they traveled north of the Indian's pigment source, they happened upon the breathtaking Sycamore Canyon, whose water flows into the Verde River. This canyon provided them with the gold treasure that their country had been seeking for so many years. After detailing its location on a map, the Spaniards returned to Mexico City, burdened with a carefree load of samples of their newfound mineral.

Surprisingly, Espejo and his expedition were denied access to the entire area when they attempted to make their return trip. The Sycamore Canyon Mine laid untouched, save for unaware passersby, until 1720. Finally, the mine would be reactivated by Spanish priests, who worked the gold deposits for several years until the territorial Indians chased them away. Dormant again, the mine would no longer have to share its gold due to Indian control.

Both in 1853 and in 1873, the mine was rediscovered by various American prospectors who admired both the Spanish relics and the gold, but on both occurrences they were pursued by Indians. As years created a buffer between Indian hostility and peace, these same prospectors from the nineteenth century discoveries once again journeyed to Sycamore Canyon. But on this occasion, the mine was nowhere to be found. The Indians had permanently sealed it and hidden it from the outside world. The Sycamore Canyon Mine remains hidden to this day.

Who:_____

What:_____

Where:_____

How:_____

Others:_____

Records/Relatives:_____

Tax/Death/Military:_____

Newspapers:_____

    Internet:_____

    Sources:_____

COMMENTS:_____

_____

_____

_____

_____

_____

_____

_____

_____

Who:_____

What:_____

Where:_____

How:_____

Others:_____

Records/Relatives:_____

Tax/Death/Military:_____

Newspapers:_____

Internet:_____

Sources:_____

COMMENTS:_____

_____

_____

_____

_____

_____

_____

_____

_____

_____

Who:_____

What:_____

Where:_____

How:_____

Others:_____

Records/Relatives:_____

Tax/Death/Military:_____

Newspapers:_____

    Internet:_____

    Sources:_____

COMMENTS:_____

_____

_____

_____

_____

_____

_____

_____

_____

_____

Who:_____

What:_____

Where:_____

How:_____

Others:_____

Records/Relatives:_____

Tax/Death/Military:_____

Newspapers:_____

    Internet:_____

    Sources:_____

COMMENTS:_____

_____

_____

_____

_____

_____

_____

_____

_____

_____

Who:_____

What:_____

Where:_____

How:_____

Others:_____

Records/Relatives:_____

Tax/Death/Military:_____

Newspapers:_____

    Internet:_____

    Sources:_____

COMMENTS:_____

_____

_____

_____

_____

_____

_____

_____

_____

_____

Who:_____

What:_____

Where:_____

How:_____

Others:_____

Records/Relatives:_____

Tax/Death/Military:_____

Newspapers:_____

    Internet:_____

    Sources:_____

COMMENTS:_____

_____

_____

_____

_____

_____

_____

_____

_____

NOTES

_____

_____

_____

_____

_____

_____

_____

_____

_____

_____

_____

_____

_____

_____

_____

_____

_____

_____

_____

_____

_____

_____

NOTES

NOTES

_____

_____

_____

_____

_____

_____

_____

_____

_____

_____

_____

_____

_____

_____

_____

_____

_____

_____

NOTES

NOTES

NOTES

NOTES

NOTES

NOTES

NOTES

CHAPTER FIFTEEN

ARIZONA

THE TREASURE OF HERMAN WOLF

THE TREASURE OF HERMAN WOLF

In 1864, the American government, via their soldiers, began arresting members of the tribe of Navajo Indians. When that occurred, many of the Navajo families escaped into the caves of Canyon Diablo to hide and elude capture by the troops. After the massive wave of arrests, there were eighty thousand Navajo Indians incarcerated for four years at Fort Sumner, New Mexico. The military members confiscated all of their land and animals.

During the Civil War, these arrests were temporarily suspended, but when the war ended, the soldiers began the Indian roundup once again. Post-war, in 1867, the first battle took place at Canyon Diablo. A common beaver trader by the name of Wolf was also in the Canyon Diablo region; he was building an elaborate trading post on the river downstream from the mouth of the canyon. Along with his work on that project, he was assisting the cavalry in their fight against the rebel Indians.

The Navajo Indians were not aware of his connection with the military, so when most of the tribe was released from their prison sentences in 1868, they headed to the Little Colorado River basin and his trading post, believing this white man could offer them protection. Once there they settled further south into their old camps along Canyon Diablo.

Wolf was an extremely wise businessman and cautious with the profits from his trading post and so he buried most of them to avoid theft, which was still common throughout the end of the nineteenth century. Consistently, he packed gold and silver coins into small cans and jars and interred them close to the fence posts around his property. He operated his trading post on the Little Colorado River over thirty years' time and had accumulated an estimate estate of over $350,000. The entire amount is believed to consist of thousands of gold and silver coins.

In 1901, twenty American gold coins were uncovered near the Little Colorado River; and in 1966, a bucket of Mexican silver coins was discovered near the same location. These have been the only two discoveries over the years relating to this treasure, and are expected to be a minimal percentage of what was actually buried. The Wolf Trading Post treasure has never been found and is expected to still be in the Canyon Diablo region, near the Little Colorado River, just off the California-Santa Fe Trail. The site is located on the current Navajo Indian Reservation, south of Tolchico, in Coconino County, Arizona.

Who:_____

What:_____

Where:_____

How:_____

Others:_____

Records/Relatives:_____

Tax/Death/Military:_____

Newspapers:_____

    Internet:_____

    Sources:_____

COMMENTS:_____

_____

_____

_____

_____

_____

_____

_____

_____

_____

Who:_____

What:_____

Where:_____

How:_____

Others:_____

Records/Relatives:_____

Tax/Death/Military:_____

Newspapers:_____

    Internet:_____

    Sources:_____

COMMENTS:_____

_____

_____

_____

_____

_____

_____

_____

_____

_____

Who:_____

What:_____

Where:_____

How:_____

Others:_____

Records/Relatives:_____

Tax/Death/Military:_____

Newspapers:_____

Internet:_____

Sources:_____

COMMENTS:_____

_____

_____

_____

_____

_____

_____

_____

_____

_____

Who:_____

What:_____

Where:_____

How:_____

Others:_____

Records/Relatives:_____

Tax/Death/Military:_____

Newspapers:_____

    Internet:_____

    Sources:_____

COMMENTS:_____

_____

_____

_____

_____

_____

_____

_____

_____

_____

Who:_____

What:_____

Where:_____

How:_____

Others:_____

Records/Relatives:_____

Tax/Death/Military:_____

Newspapers:_____

    Internet:_____

    Sources:_____

COMMENTS:_____

_____

_____

_____

_____

_____

_____

_____

_____

_____

Who:_____

What:_____

Where:_____

How:_____

Others:_____

Records/Relatives:_____

Tax/Death/Military:_____

Newspapers:_____

    Internet:_____

    Sources:_____

COMMENTS:_____

_____

_____

_____

_____

_____

_____

_____

_____

_____

NOTES

NOTES

NOTES

_____

_____

_____

_____

_____

_____

_____

_____

_____

_____

_____

_____

_____

_____

_____

_____

_____

_____

_____

NOTES

NOTES

_____

_____

_____

_____

_____

_____

_____

_____

_____

_____

_____

_____

_____

_____

_____

_____

_____

_____

_____

NOTES

NOTES

_____
_____
_____
_____
_____
_____
_____
_____
_____
_____
_____
_____
_____
_____
_____
_____
_____
_____

NOTES

NOTES

_____

_____

_____

_____

_____

_____

_____

_____

_____

_____

_____

_____

_____

_____

_____

_____

_____

_____

_____

NOTES

CHAPTER SIXTEEN

ARIZONA

SKELETON CANYON

SKELETON CANYON

During the nineteenth century, Skeleton Canyon was used as a secret passage to transport money and goods into the United States from Mexico. Both Mexican and American smugglers would travel the route and sell their transported items on the black market. Skeleton Canyon is situated in southeast Arizona, just a stone's throw from both the New Mexico and Mexico borders.

In July, 1881 in Mexico, a troop of bandits called the Estrada Gang had just plundered the town of Monterrey. As they discussed plans to transport their newfound loot into America through Skeleton Canyon, they didn't realize that an American thief was nearby and listening to their conversation. The American was Jim Hughes; he frequented high crime areas such as Charleston and Galeyville, Arizona and Shakespeare, New Mexico.

Armed with enough information to intercept the delivery, Hughes traveled back to Arizona to inform his gang of their upcoming robbery. He knew if they were able to launch a surprise attack on the Estrada Gang, the accompanying treasure would be easy to steal. He strategized with William "Curly Bill" Brocius, Billy Clanton of Tombstone, and Newton Hayes Clanton. These criminals were convinced their plan was a gold mine.

As they finalized their attack plan, their spies related crucial information the Estrada Gang was coming through the canyon earlier than expected. Since Curly Bill was not in town for the raid, Hughes found two other friends to assist in his place, namely Zwing Hunt and Billy Grounds. The Estrada Gang came into an area called Devil's Kitchen where they postponed their trip to eat and have a siesta. Under the spies' watchful eyes, the gang was seen with no less than thirty heavily packed mules.

Once they all fell asleep, Hughes and his bandits let loose with a concert of gunfire. The Estrada Gang didn't have any way to escape the bloodbath that raged around them that day. As the mules ran off due to the loud gunshots, they were shot as well so as not to escape with the loot.

As the smoke finished wafting through the air, the resulting scene was horrific. Nineteen members of the Mexican gang and twenty-six mules lay dead. The Americans quickly collected $75,000 in coins, jewels, and artifacts, but were soon dismayed to realize they had no way to carry the treasure out of the canyon. Their small numbers of horses were unable to carry such a great weight. Instead, they each carried a small amount and buried the rest in Skeleton Canyon, to return to at a later time. They were home within days to spend the small fortune they each had transported.

Always one to deceive and double-cross, Hughes concocted another plan with Hunt and Grounds. While he remained in Galeyville, so as not to look suspicious, Hunt and Grounds would return to the canyon, dig up the treasure, and rebury it in a different location. They would then each have one third of the treasure all for themselves. Hunt and Grounds headed toward the canyon once again, but this time they deceived Hughes. They reburied the treasure and went into hiding for four months, without telling Hughes of the new location.

The two men died soon after, killed by Indians. But this did not happen until Grounds had written at least ten letters to his sister Maggie Clinger in San Antonio, Texas, describing the location of the hidden treasure.

240

Hunt is also said to have passed a treasure map on to his uncle before he died.

Hunt's map showed the treasure was buried at the base of Davis Mountain. However, Davis Mountain was a name that only they used, it is not an official mountain in Arizona. It is believed today to be one of the Peloncilla Mountains.

The map also explained that there was a curving canyon near Davis Mountain with an east wall of rocks and a west wall of forest. Walking through this canyon would lead you to a stream with a ten foot drop. At the bottom of the drop were to be two springs and a three feet high square-shaped rock. Twenty steps west of the rock were where the treasure was buried.

Armed with these letters and clues, the Hunt family searched for the buried treasure for years. They were unable to even find the two springs, let alone the treasure. Over the years, it is believed that earthquakes and extreme weather could have relocated or dried up any springs, streams, or rocks. The treasure of Skeleton Canyon remains to be found.

Who:_____

What:_____

Where:_____

How:_____

Others:_____

Records/Relatives:_____

Tax/Death/Military:_____

Newspapers:_____

Internet:_____

Sources:_____

COMMENTS:_____

_____

_____

_____

_____

_____

_____

_____

_____

_____

Who:_____

What:_____

Where:_____

How:_____

Others:_____

Records/Relatives:_____

Tax/Death/Military:_____

Newspapers:_____

    Internet:_____

    Sources:_____

COMMENTS:_____

_____

_____

_____

_____

_____

_____

_____

_____

_____

Who:_____

What:_____

Where:_____

How:_____

Others:_____

Records/Relatives:_____

Tax/Death/Military:_____

Newspapers:_____

Internet:_____

Sources:_____

COMMENTS:_____

_____

_____

_____

_____

_____

_____

_____

_____

_____

Who:_____

What:_____

Where:_____

How:_____

Others:_____

Records/Relatives:_____

Tax/Death/Military:_____

Newspapers:_____

    Internet:_____

    Sources:_____

COMMENTS:_____

_____

_____

_____

_____

_____

_____

_____

_____

_____

Who:_____

What:_____

Where:_____

How:_____

Others:_____

Records/Relatives:_____

Tax/Death/Military:_____

Newspapers:_____

    Internet:_____

    Sources:_____

COMMENTS:_____

_____

_____

_____

_____

_____

_____

_____

_____

Who:_____

What:_____

Where:_____

How:_____

Others:_____

Records/Relatives:_____

Tax/Death/Military:_____

Newspapers:_____

Internet:_____

Sources:_____

COMMENTS:_____

_____

_____

_____

_____

_____

_____

_____

_____

_____

NOTES

NOTES

_____

_____

_____

_____

_____

_____

_____

_____

_____

_____

_____

_____

_____

_____

_____

_____

_____

_____

_____

NOTES

NOTES

NOTES

NOTES

_____
_____
_____
_____
_____
_____
_____
_____
_____
_____
_____
_____
_____
_____
_____
_____
_____
_____

NOTES

NOTES

_____

_____

_____

_____

_____

_____

_____

_____

_____

_____

_____

_____

_____

_____

_____

_____

_____

_____

_____

_____

NOTES

NOTES

CHAPTER SEVENTEEN

ARIZONA

LA PURISIMA CONCEPION MINE

LA PURISIMA CONCEPION MINE

Catholic priests of the Jesuit order were heavily concentrated in populations of the American Southwest with their church members, the Spanish explorers. The highest concentrations of priests were found in what is now Southern Arizona.

Originally founded by Indians, the southwestern mines were so desirable that the conquistadores came in and drove the tribes out of the area. The Spaniards worked the mines for several years and allowed access to the Jesuits. Although the Jesuits witnessed great treasure while in the region, including gold, silver, bullion bars, coins, and ores, they were forbidden to take anything when forced out, with their conquistador counterparts, by the Indians.

When the Indians returned, they destroyed the openings and disallowed entry to the mines. The treasure troves were now "lost" but the Jesuits had kept records. Ancient Jesuit documents detail clues that possibly lead to the Immaculate Conception Mine, also called La Purisima Concepcion.

It is perhaps the richest and most elusive gold and silver mine ever worked by the Indians of Arizona. The ore taken from this mine is said to be so rich that one needed 12 arrastres to crush it and it would yield ½ silver and ½ gold. Slabs of silver weighing between 25 and 50 pounds each were available with minimal work for the miner.

The clues read as follows:

1. Go straight and true through the pass of Los Janos, south 3 leagues from the mine of nuestra senora de Guadalupe. This mine is but one league from the big gate of the Mision de Tumucacori.

2. From there go to another paso called Agua Hondo. To the south from this pass lies a creek that empties itself on the desert near the village of Santa Cruz.

3. The mine lies just east of Agua Hondo and near the banks of the creek. Here you will see many arrastres and patios for crushing the ore. Above these lies a tunnel 300 varas long.

4. In the rock above this tunnel is carved the name of the mine, the words "La Purisima Concepcion". The mouth of the tunnel is covered by a door of copper fastened with a large iron lock.

5. To the west of this tunnel is a crosscut nearly 100 varas long. The ore here is yellow in color and bears four fifths silver and one fifth gold.

6. Fifty varas south from the mouth of the mine will be found many slabs of silver and some of gold. These weigh 25-50 pounds each.

The location is estimated to be in a narrow pass in the western end of the El Pajarito Mountains, near Cerro Ruido Mountain, thirteen miles southwest of Tumacacori Mission in Santa Cruz County. It is likewise very close to the Mexican border.

Who:_____

What:_____

Where:_____

How:_____

Others:_____

Records/Relatives:_____

Tax/Death/Military:_____

Newspapers:_____

    Internet:_____

    Sources:_____

COMMENTS:_____

_____

_____

_____

_____

_____

_____

_____

_____

_____

Who:_____

What:_____

Where:_____

How:_____

Others:_____

Records/Relatives:_____

Tax/Death/Military:_____

Newspapers:_____

    Internet:_____

    Sources:_____

COMMENTS:_____

_____

_____

_____

_____

_____

_____

_____

_____

_____

Who:_____

What:_____

Where:_____

How:_____

Others:_____

Records/Relatives:_____

Tax/Death/Military:_____

Newspapers:_____

    Internet:_____

    Sources:_____

COMMENTS:_____

_____

_____

_____

_____

_____

_____

_____

_____

_____

_____

Who:_____

What:_____

Where:_____

How:_____

Others:_____

Records/Relatives:_____

Tax/Death/Military:_____

Newspapers:_____

Internet:_____

Sources:_____

COMMENTS:_____

_____

_____

_____

_____

_____

_____

_____

_____

Who:_____

What:_____

Where:_____

How:_____

Others:_____

Records/Relatives:_____

Tax/Death/Military:_____

Newspapers:_____

    Internet:_____

    Sources:_____

COMMENTS:_____

_____

_____

_____

_____

_____

_____

_____

_____

_____

Who:_____

What:_____

Where:_____

How:_____

Others:_____

Records/Relatives:_____

Tax/Death/Military:_____

Newspapers:_____

    Internet:_____

    Sources:_____

COMMENTS:_____

_____

_____

_____

_____

_____

_____

_____

_____

_____

NOTES

_____

_____

_____

_____

_____

_____

_____

_____

_____

_____

_____

_____

_____

_____

_____

_____

_____

_____

_____

_____

NOTES

NOTES

_____

_____

_____

_____

_____

_____

_____

_____

_____

_____

_____

_____

_____

_____

_____

_____

_____

_____

_____

_____

NOTES

NOTES

_____

_____

_____

_____

_____

_____

_____

_____

_____

_____

_____

_____

_____

_____

_____

_____

_____

_____

_____

_____

NOTES

NOTES

NOTES

NOTES

_____

_____

_____

_____

_____

_____

_____

_____

_____

_____

_____

_____

_____

_____

_____

_____

_____

_____

_____

_____

_____

_____

NOTES

Manufactured by Amazon.ca
Acheson, AB